BURNOUT – WHAT'S NEXT?

Solutions for High-Performer Burnout

BURNOUT – WHAT'S NEXT?
Solutions for High-Performer Burnout!

I would like to dedicate this book to everyone that has helped me on my journey as an act of love and my desire to share with you the knowledge I've gained.

I would like to dedicate this book to all of those I have had an opportunity to work with and learn from because it is through these experiences that I have achieved my personal growth, dreams and goals. Events in this book are my own experiences and I am grateful to everyone that I have worked with over the years, contributing to these experiences.

I pledge to share my experiences and tools with authenticity and without apology. I know that I can provide others with gifts of hope, wisdom, tools and joy in speaking about my experience. I pledge that I will continue to work to gain clarity and focus for my readers, audiences, and clients. Then, I can continue to make the world a better place, one word at a time.

INTRODUCTION

Sometimes we are forced to build awareness, resilience, and support to find the roots of the burnout and solutions that will help us navigate a successful and satisfying life.

This book is for high achievers who want to break the walls that we create in our minds, and therefore, our lives. Break free from limitations that we are pre-programmed to a new possibility in life and business.

THIS BOOK IS FOR YOU:

- If you are looking for a new direction in life

- If you're feeling frustrated, stressed, or even angry about your work

- If your performance on the job and your relationships at work or home are suffering

- If your business failed

- If no matter how hard you've tried, you can't see a way to get "unstuck"

- If stress is high, and you don't know where to turn or what to do

If you feel like you need some support, i.e., you want people to believe in what you're doing and want people to believe in your vision.

As they say, knowledge is power, but without taking specific actions to prevent and reverse stress and burnout, you won't enjoy the success, no matter how much you want to.

I give you a practical, step-by-step guide to transforming your life while putting these decisive steps into action in relationships and business.

Burnout may follow, significantly affecting the individual's and organization's ability to function.

Cumulative stress is familiar to those working in conflict and post-conflict areas. It often relates to a combination of factors: time pressure, heavy workload, the mindset of leaders and employees, multinational culture, long hours, uncomfortable or dangerous conditions, need for decisions with inadequate information and communication, confusion over responsibilities, lack of support, ineffective leadership, conflicting priorities, insufficient preparation or unclear goals, personality types, styles, interpersonal conflicts and inadequate attention to stress management strategies.

On Jul 31, 2019, the World Health Organization accepted burnout as a medical condition. Scientifically it has been proven that emotional avoidance is a common reaction to trauma.

The tools provided in this book have helped many I coached. I hope to help you as well in how to respond to a situation we never imagined encountering!

I am writing this book for you! Whatever comes your way, you are not alone, and you are never powerless. Love for life and people is the most potent force in this universe, and based on that, we can build anything! It is the structure foundation that will build you up for lifelong success.

After reading this book, you will understand how to change your life and transform it for lifelong success. You will learn:

Applicable solutions and steps for High-Performer Burnout!

Discover your genetics of burnout and operating systems

Find your blind spots and coping mechanisms

Your relating and adapting style

Know your DNA – inner guidance genius

Align your character, your dispute, your tribe

Evaluate your strengths; rephrase, renew, rebuild

Think to reach a high achievement level without burning out

These action steps will serve anyone to be unbreakable in any situation and build success in any business or relationships.

CONTENTS

- Relating and Adapting – How to Win with the Determination of Your Soul

- Essentials of Leadership – Character and Disputes

- Align with the Whole – Fight the Ego

PART III – Page 105

OPEN TO NEW POSSIBILITIES

- How to Make Smart Choices and Manage Your Outcomes

- Hot to Find the Beauty in Everyone

- The Gift of Saying "NO" is not Against Others; it's For You.

- The Only Person You Should Change is You

- Leverage the Curiosity and Drive Success

- Integrity Within

- The 'Attitude of Gratitude' Operating System

- Know How Powerful You Are – Leverage this Power

PART I

THE BURNOUT THAT WE SHOULD AVOID AT ANY COST!

Instead of Thinking Outside the Box, Get Rid of the Box.
– Deepak Chopra

Many books and articles exist about burnout; however, I wasn't aware of this information as I was always too busy with an everyday, endless to-do list. The funny part is that I was not aware of what I needed the most. I found out that burnout is a slow process built up over time, and often, we are not aware it is happening.

Many factors cause burnout, and in my case, it was a combination of personality type, emotional exhaustion, unhealthy habits, and a fixed perspective paradigm. Fortunately, I had a responsible job that I loved, which helped keep me sane. But the downside of being a high achiever meant that I had more responsibilities than I could handle and it made me feel stretched in all directions. I didn't know how to say "NO." On top of that, from my background, living under a Communist dictatorship, I did not take the advice I received from my friends and coworkers.

I took care of my sick son, born with extreme food allergies and eczema, spent many hours in emergency rooms and hospitals, which included many near-death experiences. Besides, my ex-husband developed bladder cancer and spent a long time suffering until he recovered from cancer, and then had open-heart surgery, which I helped him with until he recovered. I have also always helped my parents and sisters.

One day, I could not handle things any longer; even when love knocked on my door, I was too blind to see! The stress level was so high that I could not think straight. I hit the wall, and my life crumbled right in front of my eyes.

I divorced, sold my home, left the job that I loved, fought with my family, and lived with my teenage son, not knowing how to pay rent or buy food. I got too sick with an autoimmune disease and was in and out of the emergency room. One time, almost dying, I saw myself lying in the hospital bed and life fading away; unconsciously, I saw the other side, Heaven!

I lived in a world of blame and complaints, anger, fear, anxiety, self-doubt, not being good enough, low vibration, should and should-not, and shortcomings.

With the help of my faithful friends, I went deep within myself. I tirelessly studied and experimented with myself and found the solutions for burnout.

I learned the principles of mindfulness and how to apply them in everyday life. Meditation helped me switch from the fight-or-flight mode to clarity and building awareness of the way of being, doing, and having.

I began to walk outside every day. I studied endlessly — with books, conferences, classes, programs, videos, audios, and articles — to learn from the best in the self-help field.

To heal, I needed to make a self-discovery and reach the point where I could see myself clearly and become self-aware of the many limiting beliefs and shortcomings I had.

We all have these blind spots of which we're not aware. I asked for help and found a mentor who helped me overcome all my problems.

My advice is not to try to do this alone, as I found out that we don't know what we don't know. It would help if you worked with a coach; he or she is an objective observer who can take a critical look at why you have issues; and what will motivate, inspire, and challenge you to be your best. The coach will recognize your limitations and help you to see them too. Through this process, you will gain clarity, discipline, and commitment to take the necessary actions and steps to achieve greatness.

CHAPTER 1

The Genetics of Burnout – How We are Wired When We're Born

We Are Born to Die – The Difference is the Intensity With Which We Choose to Live!
— Gina Lollobrigida

Let's start with a question: How do you feel when you have no idea how to come out from stress and the mess of burnout? Let's start from the root of the problem. Our DNA! The environment that we were born in set the stage and built the DNA of how our life will play out. Unfortunately, most of the time we operate on autopilot. All analyses of ethnic and culture-specific patterns from disadvantaged backgrounds and psychosocial backgrounds raise the risk factors for stress that influence our health. Consequences of stress, especially on women before/during/after pregnancy, affect our children's future based on women's biology, medical background, psychosocial factors, and individual personality type.

Studies have shown that chronic stress on moms affect their children and can cause several physical symptoms like sleep problems, digestive issues, headaches, muscle tension, and high blood pressure. A dynamic and critical period where the various environmental factors, stress, infection, and malnutrition are associated with an increased risk for neurological disorders such as autism, schizophrenia, and Attention Deficit Hyperactivity Disorder. I experienced firsthand my daughter's miscarriage; my son was born with severe allergies and eczema where in the first five years of his life he couldn't lie down on the bed as he could not breathe. All this because I was under tremendous stress at that time. He experienced several near-death conditions. Later, I discovered he developed ADHD. That journey and many events include the closed mindset that sent me into a total burnout! Therefore, I must educate and spread the message to help as many people as I can!

Here is the thought process that affects our wellbeing:

1. The brain regularly scans for real or perceived threats; information is filtered through the limbic system, where we instinctively react with "fight, flight or freeze" based on previous experiences registered in our brain.

2. When a threat is perceived, the amygdala alerts the hypothalamus to release stress hormones, and alarms the sympathetic nervous system to fight, flight, or freeze.

3. The reaction to the "fight, flight or freeze" response creates fear, frustration, and heartache, which influence the mind, resulting in unrealistic decisions, choices, and reactions.

4. Before childhood and adulthood, trauma increases the brain-body responses. With prior trauma, the parasympathetic nervous system automatically activates, resulting in numbing or dissociating.

5. The reaction occurs because your body thinks it's in "fight or flight" mode. You produce a surge of stress hormones, which affects your baby's stress management system.

CLARIFYING QUESTIONS

There are common questions that reveal when you are prone to stress/anxiety/burnout:

- Do you find that you are prone to negative thinking about your job?

- Do you find that you are more challenging and less sympathetic to people than perhaps they deserve?

- Do you find yourself getting irritated by small problems or by your coworker and team?

- Do you feel misunderstood or unappreciated by your coworkers?

- Do you feel that you have no one to talk to or trust?

- Do you feel that you are achieving less than you should?

- Do you feel under an unpleasant level of pressure to succeed?

- Do you feel that you are not getting what you want out of your job?

- Do you feel that you are in the wrong organization or the wrong profession?

- Are you becoming frustrated with parts of your job?

- Do you feel that there is more work to do than you practically can do?

- Do you feel that you do not have time to do many critical things to do a good quality job?

- Do you find that you do not have time to plan as much as you would like?

- Do you feel run-down and drained of physical or emotional energy?

- Are you blaming and complaining?

- Do you have negative self-talk or a negative self-image?

- What is your irritability stressor?

- Are you attached vs. committed?

- How do you react to criticism?

- How do you handle a difficult situation?

ACTION STEPS

- Build a routine to save yourself time.

- Be self-aware, and jot down thoughts that keep you up at night; sometimes, getting them down on paper can make you take a more proactive approach to solve problems.

- You may also want to consider yoga; it's not only relaxing, but a great way to stay fit and healthy.

- The important thing is to find something that works for you – even if it's as simple as closing your eyes and taking a few deep breaths or taking a quick walk at lunch to clear your mind.

- It's important to know yourself and your limits.

- If you start to experience symptoms you can't shake, you should let your doctor know.

- Be aware of what standards you hold yourself to; high expectations for work or relationships.

- Find a mentor to improve social relationships at home and the office to improve health and well-being.

- Stressed parents are less responsive to their children's cues, and that less-sensitive caregiving is stressful to babies/children. Everyone has some stress. How you deal with it can help your baby's emotional growth.

- A pressing deadline at work or a one-time disagreement with your partner may get your heart rate up, but they do not typically cause long-term worry for your baby. If you're able to get past the stress and not linger there, you're golden.

- Significant life changes, such as a death in the family, divorce, or losing your job or home, affect our wellbeing.

- Long-term hardships such as financial problems, health issues, abuse, or depression.

- Disasters including hurricanes, earthquakes, or other unexpected traumatic events.

- Exposure to racism and everyday difficulties faced by being in a minority group.

- Severe stress about pregnancy, your baby's health, and caring for your baby.

- The environment has a significant impact on everything that we do. Be aware of the toxic environment we are in, and move on.

- Build awareness and a growth mindset as they will help you along away; as we know, everyone does the best from their level of awareness.

Just like we all maintain a certain level of physical health which fluctuates and changes, mental health is equally subject to change! The trouble is, we're not taught how to recognize these issues.

From a young age, we're taught to remember and talk about the signs and symptoms of the flu and other common physical illnesses. Still, it's incredibly unusual to get the same insights and training in understanding the development of mental health issues. Because of the individual nature of mental health and mental health issues, it can become increasingly difficult to identify and treat correctly. As such, the importance of cultivating self-awareness and a healthy routine of positive mental health practices is enormous.

In times of stress, start by asking yourself these questions:

1. What is causing me this stress? Be as specific as possible.

2. Can I actively do anything to change the situation; through meditation, deep breathing, exercise, or music? To whom I explain my situation and get insights?

3. If I can make changes, do I have the motivation to do so? If not, am I willing to accept the results of nothing changing?

These are just some ways to confront your mental health blockages and how you combat the first signs of stress:

- Go to a quiet place, close your eyes, and take a deep breath in and out six times.

- Ask yourself why you are feeling this way.

- Write down everything that you feel and think.

- We know that we cannot have a single feeling without first thinking about it. Check for any toxic thoughts, as the toxic thoughts are harmful to your body!

- Write down who is involved in the issue or what it is about; evaluate your judgment.

- Ask yourself a question: what was my input in that situation?

- Evaluate your perceptions as they could be wrong.

- Most of the time, situations are out of your control. What is in your possession is only your response. Respond positively to get the results you want.

- Practice forgiveness as we know "to forgive is given for," so practice compassion.

- Gain control over your thinking, behaviors, and images to create the result you want.

- Simple changes in your thoughts change your life, as we know everything first is thought and then is a thing.

- Take ownership of your feelings and outcomes. It is a key to personal development without self-judgment or blaming and complaining about others or events.

- Meditate every day for 20 minutes in the morning and 20 minutes before you sleep, as it gives the brain relaxation and clarity to switch from the fight-or-flight mode.

- Remember, when someone says something to you that hurts, look inside yourself and see what you are telling yourself about yourself!

- Remember that what might look useful to you might not look right to the other person. It is just your perception that creates your judgment. Listen to understand; observe; verify your thoughts; evaluate your observations.

- Listen to uplifting music and walk outside. It will give you perspective and heal the soul.

- Drink water so your brain is working correctly. Stay connected with your tribe.

There are three things that are extremely tough; one of them is to know one's self. It's up to us to make the necessary changes and adjust! I can come back powerfully into the high performer without burning out, so you can too!

CHAPTER 2

Our Cultural Expectations

We Blame Society, But We Are Society!

Why do disputes happen between people with different personal cultures?

We are the product of the unique culture that we build from the moment we are born. We picked it up from our parents, siblings, teachers, friends, neighbors, bosses, coworkers, media, language, and traditions. As a result, we create and have the reference point for good or bad, and we have our expectations and preferences. We comply with our family culture, city culture, organizational culture, and country's culture. Therefore, we create our own identity based on our perception of our own culture, and we compare ourselves with the world! We are aware or not; everywhere we go, we bring our piece of culture and adjust to every situation, relationship, or experience.

I've coached executives from the US, China, Russia, Korea, India, Turkey, Albania, and South America. I found out the significant problems come from their cultural awareness, communication, and relationship management styles. A common problem in many cross-cultural situations is that we compare communication styles to what we're accustomed to and then judge against them. If behaviors aren't what we consider 'normal,' we're often quick to assign questionable or even poor intent to those behaviors. At an early age, I learned that I had to adjust my style of interacting with members from other cultures, ethnicities, and backgrounds in my new workplace. Developing a foundational knowledge of those cultural differences and striving to suspend judgment as you encounter feedback styles that may be far more direct — or indirect — than you're accustomed to can make the difference between helpful or hurtful evaluations of a team member. Be open minded, as this is difficult for us as humans because we're wired to jump to conclusions about everything. When we encounter something we don't consider 'normal,' our immediate reflex is to reject that behavior or judge it somehow. Still, you need to be aware that there are various behaviors and beliefs within different countries and regions. While negative feedback can be challenging to hear, these cultures' intent usually isn't to hurt you. The feedback delivered in a way that's considered constructive by the other person is acceptable by any culture.

These steps helped me and many other executives to build our emotional intelligence and upgrade our mindset:

- Self-awareness. Understanding one's natural tendencies is an essential first step. Where is your comfort zone?

- Learn, adapt, practice. Once you know your natural tendencies, you can develop a micro-behavior portfolio to address the tensions you don't manage well.

- Contextual awareness. It is becoming a more effective means of expanding your current approach to incorporate new behaviors and knowing when to focus more on one side of the tension or the other. It requires both contextual awareness and emotional intelligence, sourced directly from the surrounding social environment.

- Be better by making a note of cultural nuances and acting accordingly on communicating across cultures.

- Get insights and get to the root of why the other person is acting in a particular manner.

- Be a good listener. Let others know you are interested in them and not coming from a place of authority or judgment. Observe and reflect.

- Being aware of the language you use with genuine curiosity, humility, and vulnerability can go a long way.

- Treat everyone with respect, which means "to look again." It's essential to look at people from new angles to want to know and learn from them.

- Above all, speak from the heart. Seek first to understand, then to be understood.

- Practice compassion: everybody has their good and bad days, especially at this drastic shift. When a coworker is having a rough time, has missed a deadline, or does something out of character, don't immediately dismiss them.

- Practice this by fostering an environment of openness with your colleagues. Be open about when you're having a hard time.

- Had a late night helping your kid with homework? Start with that when you come in that morning and apologize in advance for any aloofness that day.

- Foster trust with your colleagues by being transparent when you share updates and feedback.

- Even if you're not the one in charge, practice transparency by explaining your decisions, making yourself available for questions, and responding positively to honest feedback.

- Communication, once again, plays a significant role. Make it a point to encourage face-to-face communication within your office so that everyone feels like they're on the same page.

- Approachable and humble executives are the kind of leaders that most employees want to see at their workplace.

- Collaborate with others whenever possible, especially if you feel that you can learn from them. When you do, make sure that they know you appreciate them for contributing.

- While it's essential to hold yourself or other people accountable, checking in too often and correcting too many little mistakes will make it seem as though you don't trust your or their judgment.

- Practice active listening. Many people listen only to respond, which can leave the speaker feeling unheard.

- Remember, you're not listening to respond; you're listening to learn something new.

- Don't jump to conclusions about the things that other people say; instead, ask questions.

- You're never going to please everyone, and when someone has an issue with your leadership style, listen to it.

- You might disagree with what they're saying, but that doesn't mean that's it's not entirely unreasonable — at the very least, you'll learn something about perspective!

- Be mindful of your words. Always be aware of what you're saying and who is listening.

- Look at mistakes as lessons and rejections as a blessing in disguise.

- I have a clear understanding of my emotions and how I react to difficult situations.

- I understand the "triggers" and "stressors" in my life and plan to process stress and disappointment.

- I continue to stay curious and frequently take steps to learn more about myself.

- When I receive criticism, I ask: "How can I learn from this experience?"

- I have a clear understanding of how I react in different environments.

- I tailor the way I provide feedback to others based on their innate behavioral drives and needs.

- I regularly ask others to give me feedback about my actions, communication, and management style.

- I'm aware of the non-verbal cues I give to the people I work with.

- I'm aware of my tone of voice when I'm speaking to others in the workplace.

- I defer judgment and allow others to finish their thoughts before responding.

- I use behavioral assessment tools to identify my innate strengths and areas I need to work on.

- I use behavioral assessment tools to understand the best way to motivate and manage my direct reports.

- I have completed a 360-degree review to gather honest feedback from coworkers, family, direct reports, and managers.

When I make vital decisions, I write down what I expect will happen; nine months to a year later, I compare the results to my expectations.

CHAPTER 3

How to Be Aware & Overcome Our Blind Spots

There are three things extremely hard: steel, a diamond, and to know one's self.
— Benjamin Franklin

Burnout does not happen overnight. It is a slow process and overcoming it will be a well-structured process that will depend on how open you are to embrace change. Our perception and operating system allow us to view reality and relationships from our perspective. Have you noticed that when you ask five different people when an accident happens, you get five other descriptions, meaning five different perceptions; and sometimes our perception is wrong? In that case, we give our brain incorrect information. Then we build an attitude toward it; therefore, we behave that way. In that case, our behaviors are condition-based, so when we change our perception of something, we change the behaviors that serve us, not to destroy us!

We are all made with weaknesses and strengths, and it is within our ability to choose the direction we want. Enhancing our awareness and resilience is the right path to enjoy this beautiful trip we call Life. However, to make transformational changes, you'll need full determination and commitment to replace your limiting beliefs with empowering ones. You'll need a shift in perception, which will take time and effort. Limitations affect us in many ways. One standard method is what we say to ourselves; our self-talk. Our belief system creates our paradigm in which we operate when we are in a fight-or-flight mood. The clarity and awareness of how we approach and behave in every aspect of life is a process that will serve us for a lifetime. We must identify our patterns, tendencies to do things in specific ways that do not help us any longer, and replace them, transform them into empowering and sustaining practices, and navigate the gap between the old and the new paradigm. Finding the strength and the fire within you to never give up even if you face the most unimaginable circumstances is what I call "The Power of Will." Possessing this trait can turn anyone into an unbreakable human being.

How often do we give away our ability to respond and control our outcomes to other people? We feel hurt when someone makes nasty comments or hurt our feelings. What people say to you is simply another event, and how it makes you feel is just another outcome you have the power to control. No one can make you feel anything; you can control how you feel about any situation. No one can affect your feelings unless you allow it. Liberate yourself from the sickness of mind – connect your mind, body, and spirit.

ACTION STEPS

I used the following exercise, and it helped me tremendously, and I hope to help you too!

Divide a piece of paper into two columns. On the left, write down your *old* way of being. On the right, write down the new and uplifting way of being, doing, and having.

Write down every thought or feeling you experience:

- What irritates you? What are your triggers?
- Somebody drives me nuts—my boss, my coworker, my employees, my spouse, my child.
- What is your self-talk?
- I am not good enough; I cannot handle this any longer; I will do it my way, or the highway; I am tired; I am ugly; I am not worthy.
- What do you feel strongly about?
- She is not fair with me; they are all after me; she hurt me, and I don't want to see her face.
- My employees leave me with a bad attitude, and they are so unproductive I could cry.
- How open are you to changing your perceptions and limiting beliefs?
- What do you mean? I am entirely right, and I don't want to change a thing about myself!
- What is your biggest complaint, and why?
- My coworker, my son, and my spouse take advantage of me and don't appreciate me; they don't listen, and they act so poorly with me.
- What are the most significant self-sabotaging habits you have that you want to change?
- I get angry and lose my temper; my relationship with people is sometimes the worst, but they are jerks — and they don't change and don't listen. I don't sleep at night.
- What are your fears, self-doubts, and worries?
- I fear I will lose my business, job, and relationships, and I worry that I cannot handle all of these.
- On the right side of the paper, write the new ways of being, doing, and having.

Write down every thought or feeling you experience:

- I take 100 percent responsibility for what I think, what I say, how I behave and act, as what I see starts with me.
- I understand that I need to change my perception about how I think, how I behave, and how I act, as the only person I can change is me.
- I am journaling, meditating, and using breathing techniques to be less stressed, and my thinking is precise; I can respond better to challenges and make better decisions.
- First, I need to be in a better place and think of what outcome I want to create. In that place, I am more aware of my thoughts, and I respond positively.
- Criticism is a gift because it shows me clues that I am off track, and failure is a stepping-stone for a better future.
- By being mindful, I connect with my inner wisdom and visualize positive outcomes. From that space, I respond to anyone or any event with positivity, no matter the other person's response.
- I am not my thoughts; I am not my emotions, as I know that we cannot think a thought without our bodies responding. Therefore, the emotions I feel are the result of my thoughts. When I control my thoughts, I manage my life.

For high achievers, it is best to focus your attention on what matters most. Use your unique qualities to get what you need right now. Stay open-hearted, grateful for all that you have, and count your blessings. Weakness and self-dialog can lead to more failure unless you are willing to learn to look at each failure and use it to your advantage to help propel your company/career forward.

We Are on the Same Ocean but in Different Boats, and We Share the Same Destination. We Survive, Revive, Thrive!

REQUIREMENTS TO FIGHT WEAKNESSES

Commitment, Discipline, Resilience, Action Plan

Answer these questions:

What is the essential thing in your life and why?

Which of your current friends do you feel will still be important to you ten years from now?

What did you learn as a child that has proven to be most valuable in your life?

How much do you feel you are in control of your life?

What are your strengths?

What are your weaknesses?

Where do you see yourself in five years?

Who is the person who has influenced your life the most? What is the most critical thing in your life, and why?

How would you describe your moral values?

If you could go back in time, what period of your own life would you like to revisit?

Who is your best friend, and why?

What is the best decision you ever made?

What is your biggest regret?

Gaining clarity of our thought process, self-awareness, values, and purpose are the first essential steps toward the road of recovery from our burnout! I did the work, so can you!

CHAPTER 4

Ways to Heal & Transform from Within

Appreciate, Enjoy the Evolution Road
We Call Life!
— Desi Tahiraj

Many of us live day in and day out in a world of blame, hate, complaints, misery, and pain. I was blaming and complaining about people for what happened to me. Living in that kind of world is miserable for me and everyone close to me. As humans, we tend to judge because it is more challenging to think! It is relatively easy for us to blame an event or other people, but we never think to ask ourselves what our role is in creating or allowing this situation to happen. We can't control the response of others, but we can find answers within ourselves. I ignored it when my friends were trying to help me and warning me! When I hit the wall, I blamed people or circumstances, asked why this happened to me, and judged everyone. Then I learned to be aware of my thoughts and how they affect my well-being; I get deep within myself and ask my soul what I want to experience. Deep inside me is that safe space where I can build my heaven and experience pure enlightenment. I begin to observe what thoughts come into my mind and write them down to get clarity. When clarity comes, I can experience a shift in perception. As a result, I share positive thoughts and positive energy and produce positive actions that will lead to positive results. I realized that the outside world is a reflection of my inner world. When I comprehend this way of thinking, then a shift in perception happens, allowing me to feel renewed and happy again. That's the *aha* moment we want.

> **"To not forgive is to drink a little poison each day and expect the other person to die."**
>
> **— Mary Morrissey**

I passionately took every opportunity to expand my knowledge. As I gained more clarity and awareness, I discovered that we have so many blind spots not aware of ourselves as humans. I finally opened up to the possibility of living outside the box and being more aware of my limitations and fears of the unknown. I started a long and very fulfilling journey of self-discovery, and I am so glad I did. I opened up to the possibility of being extraordinary!

Deep emotional stress, anger, and resentment can seriously damage your health. I realized that all the heart problems, high blood pressure problems, and infections resulted from my emotional pain that we call *stress*! I applied the following:

ACTION STEPS

Emotion is one of eight faculties in our mind, along with:
- Intellect
- Imagination
- Intuition
- Will
- "I" Awareness
- Physical Body
- Higher Self

When one of the above elements is out of balance, we suffer our consequences. It is as simple as that. If we don't address it in one mode, often it will come out in another. It can go physically, mentally, emotionally, or spiritually. These negative feelings can destroy any relationship and, most of all, your relationship with yourself.

Anger and resentment want to teach us something about ourselves; we could not think any thought without our body reacting. It is critical to be aware of what thoughts we choose to believe! This exercise will liberate you.

Too many of us are going through life on autopilot. Most of the time, we are unaware of the millions of opportunities and eye-opening experiences that can profoundly transform our lives!

There are many ways that you could heal yourself. One of the best ways is to educate yourself and be aware of what thought processes you have, as it has been proven that our thoughts affect us most profoundly!

Thinking is a compelling form of energy. Scientists say that our thoughts can travel at 186,000 miles per second!

Emotional pain is energy located in our subconscious mind, and without synchronizing our subconscious mind with our rational mind, we can't find the real cause of pain.

Important practical activities you can use to come back and enjoy life include:

- Deep guided meditation
- The EFT technique called Tapping
- Talk therapy with a coach or consultant
- Breathing techniques
- Helping charities
- Physical activities like hiking, swimming, riding, singing, dancing, skiing, tennis
- Learning a new language or a new musical instrument

- Travel or taking a vacation

Anything that a person can do close to their sanity is the right choice. Once you decide on an emotional healing activity, it is time to stick with it.

We, as humans, are healthy and are built to stick together and help each other. Go out in the world and show that you can do it and get back to light. An important point, but it doesn't seem very easy to know precisely where the boundaries are between self and others. To take an example: when we talk to ourselves, the question is 'who is talking to whom?' when the self talks. This practice of talking to ourselves, or to avatars of people we know, to recapitulate our thoughts inside us, seems taxing as often as it can be rewarding. Instead, use empowering self-talk that can be soothing. To say to ourselves 'I love you,' for instance, when we feel lonely and cannot sleep, appears to work. We CAN calm ourselves down using this kind of talk and music we love. In other cases, we can experience anger when we discuss with an avatar in our mind, for example, arguments we might have had with a relative or estranged colleague.

When arguments take place inside us, those, I think, can be painful. We can leave an argumentative colleague or talk him down if we are calm, but if the argument is with different parts of ourselves, we cannot escape, and what if the less peaceful side of us makes greater logical sense but drives us up the wall? What happens when our emotions are not in sync with our thoughts? Disaster. One person does not create the world that is today! Your thoughts produce your experiences with other people from the day we were born to the present moment. Be aware of this framework:

1. Sense of Belonging + Inner Peace = success and clarity in decision-making

The new VUCA world we live in: Volatile, Uncertain, Complex, Ambiguous. We are the ones that can destroy or build ourselves.

2. Passion Test = Evaluate + Test + Apply

Align your Vibe to your Tribe.

Ask for feedback or constructive criticism from your tribe because your vibe affects the tribe!

3. Running Away from Relationships

Irritability + Struggle with Pride and Expectation of Others = Dismissal. We have perpetuated busyness. Based on our perceptions, our judgments are formed.

4. Self-Awareness Consciousness

To give up the things that make me sick.

The quality of our life is the quality of the questions we ask. Kindness is the beauty of humans.

I am getting distracted, conscious walks and decisions.

Find that you are prone to negative thinking.

Worries, blame, doubts, anger, revenge, irritation, impatience, disappointment, jealousy, pessimism, hatred makes us sick.

Inner peace = success

Ask yourself:

What kind of people do you like to spend time with? What can people learn by looking at their friends?
In conversations, do you tend to talk more or listen?
When was the last time you cried? What was the reason?
What does it take for you to trust someone?
What would you never be willing to sacrifice?
What do you like best about your life?
What do you like least about your life?

Great minds discuss ideas; average minds discuss events; small minds discuss people.

When you focus on problems, you will have more questions. When you focus on possibilities, you'll have more opportunities. We are the ones that can destroy or build ourselves.

Passion, enthusiasm, happiness, and belief in yourself bring contentment. Today we live in a multicultural world. Each of us is born in a different environment, culture, language, circumstances, and how you will adapt and use the above action steps will determine your success.

CHAPTER 5

Ways to Get Past Resentment

Death is not the greatest loss in life. The greatest loss is what dies inside while still alive. Never surrender.
— Tupac Shakur

One of the best things you can do for yourself is to move past resentment. Resentment can be more painful than cancer. We know that every sickness comes from stress and continuing to neglect ourselves. Resentment is the lowest point that anyone can feel. By resenting things that have or have not happened and regretting the past, myself and the people close to me are the only ones who suffer. I look around and recognize that no one can fix the past or predict the future. The past is only a language that is stored in our memory and is not happening now. It's what I keep in my subconscious mind, and I resent, and indeed fear about tomorrow that did not occur yet, that can cripple my life. The only thing I can fix and enjoy is the present. Most of us are often not present and living fully in the precious moments of our lives. We live in fear of tomorrow, which affects us so profoundly that it makes us sick and small. When we come to a stop and listen to our soul without judgment, we reach the safest and most peaceful place to live. I ask myself what do I want to feel and experience? All the answers are within me. I don't need to be selfish, as each one of us must make this world a better place to live. It is my duty as a human to put love first. I choose to love instead of resent, and I remember that God chooses to love instead. My advice is to get out of the blaming and complaining that poison your mind, body, and spirit. Based on my childhood experiences, I see, observe, and judge reality through my lenses. I believe that I do the best possible and stroll through life looking at the world through my filters, and often I end up making the wrong choices repeatedly. I blame the outside world for my misfortunes. I understood that everything that happens in our lives happens *through* us and not *to* us. My life is the product of my actions. Happiness is a choice I make, and I shouldn't look outside for answers. Here is what I did.

- I was judging everything and everyone through my lenses. When my son took forever to finish his homework, I blamed myself.
- When something didn't come up in the way it needed, I blamed myself.
- When I got stuck in traffic, I blamed the traffic.
- When a coworker did something wrong, I blamed myself for not being there.
- When the weather was bad, I complained.
- If someone did something wrong, I judged and took it to heart.

These feelings work by tricking you into a vicious cycle where you are angry in the present, scared of what is to come, and full of resentment over the past. The reality is that my emotions like anger, resentment, hate, and fear are interconnected with my childhood experiences and suffering in living under the threat of communism that gave us so little freedom of choice. This system's limitations were embedded in me even though I was living in the U.S. Unconsciously, I was operating under the paranoid belief that I would lose my job if I did something wrong.

I was always worried about what other people would think of me. I put up a wall to prevent anyone from getting close to me because, unconsciously, I was afraid that if I let someone get close, I would get hurt. As my self-awareness level rose, I understood that the root of everything that happened to me was that I couldn't let go and forget about the suffering in my childhood. I realized that happiness is a choice and to forgive and forget, let go, live in the moment, and be in a place of gratitude is a duty for myself, my family, and my friends. If I do something wrong, or someone else does something wrong, and if I keep grudges, and I don't forgive, I live my life swallowing poison and expecting the other person to die — which is the lowest point of human experience. The only person who suffers is me! When anything happens, it is because both sides contributed to the problem.

Be a bigger person, as the word "forgive" means *give for*.

We all make mistakes. Because this is a part of the human experience, we should see the other side of the coin and understand that it is our choice to feel and be present and look forward to making positive steps with gratitude and accepting people's differences. No one can change the past; it doesn't exist any longer. The only thing I can change is now and moving forward. I take 100 percent responsibility for my life because my responses and actions will affect my experience. You have no idea what a liberating feeling I experienced when I cleared my soul of resentment. I felt empowered and energized and at the top of the world. Take heart and be The One.

ACTION STEPS

Some people can spend hours dwelling on the wrongs done to them: the injustices, the slights, the snubs, the accusations from lousy treatment. They can think of a particular instance and up comes the same feeling they had about the actual event, and they get angry all over again.

- To resent something or someone is once again feeling the fear that we live in every moment of our lives. The anger, the hurt, the humiliation, and the pain of the original experience — real or imagined — over our coworker, sibling, spouse...the list never ends as you do not see the big picture and get out of that vicious circle.
- When resentments are held onto and not healed, they form harmful beliefs and behavior patterns, where blaming and judgment now justify those behaviors, which is nonsense and not a straightforward assessment. Sadly, this then inhibits any emotional trauma resulting from the actual event having an avenue through which it will be resolved. The effect of holding onto the emotional trauma and the resentment creates further pain and dysfunction in the physical body, and our health is affected.
- The idea of no longer being supported by the thoughts and energy that we are right to be further judgmental increases our need to hold on to the resentment.
- The idea of liberating yourself from resentment eats away at self-esteem and peace of mind. Our internal health crumbles as feelings of hope are swallowed up by bitterness and blame.
- Of course, we can't always control what happened to us, especially as children, but we do have a choice as adults.
- We exercise the unique gift of wisdom to free ourselves from the most strangling thoughts and behaviors. The greatest gift that choice offers each one of us is that we can take ownership of our feelings and behaviors and therefore determine the outcome of our lives and the path that we tread.

- A life filled with resentments binds us tight and cripples any chance of creating a happy and joyful life in which we can express our true self that is loving, kind, and compassionate.
- The light that emanates from our true nature shines a path that is blessed, rewarding, and incredibly fulfilling.
- Please take a look inside yourself, see where it is coming from, and more importantly, question why without any judgment.
- Take time to explore, as sometimes holding onto resentment is a way of avoiding pain.
- Write thoughts and feelings down; talk about them, not in a blaming way, but with a willingness to see all aspects of the issue.
- Look also for the wisdom — the golden nugget of knowledge that will bring clarity, offering you the chance to determine what you will let go of and what requires more work.

Ask and reflect.

1. How do my moods affect my thoughts and decision-making?

2. How would I describe my communication style and its effect on others?

3. What traits in others bother me? Why?

4. Do I find it difficult to admit when I'm wrong? Why or why not?

5. What are my strengths? What are my weaknesses?

Use your emotional vocabulary.

When a doctor tries to diagnose a problem, he or she will ask you to describe the pain you're feeling. It works similarly with your emotions: By using specific words to express your feelings, it's easier to get to their root cause, enabling you to better deal with them.

Pause. If you feel yourself beginning to respond emotionally to a situation, take a break. If possible, go for a short walk.

Use this trick.

- Does this need to be said?

- Does this need to be said by me?

- Does this need to be said by me now?

- Will I regret not speaking up later?

- Adjust your volume.

When you communicate, your conversation partner will often react in the same style or tone you choose. If you speak in a calm, rational voice, they'll respond similarly. Yell or scream, and they start yelling and screaming, too.

Think before addressing sensitive topics.

Before revisiting a touchy topic, give careful thought about where and when to speak, to have a calm and rational discussion.

Learn from negative emotions.

If you find yourself struggling with negative emotions, ask yourself: What is this feeling telling me? Can I use this emotion to motivate me to make a change?

Learn from emotional hijacks.

An "emotional hijack" is a situation in which you completely lose control of your emotions. Often, it's a series of circumstances or events that culminate in an action that pushes you "over the edge." When you experience an emotional hijack, try to examine what happened by asking yourself:

- Why did I react the way I did?

- What would I change if I could do it again?

- What could I say to myself next time that would help me think more clearly?

Learn to say no.

It's great to be kind and helpful to others, but you have your limits. If you say yes to every request for your time and energy, you put yourself on the path to burnout. And remember, every time you say yes to something you don't want, you're saying no to the things you do want.

Ask your manager or a trusted colleague: "What's one thing you see me doing (or failing to do) that holds me back?"

Turn criticism into constructive feedback. When you receive criticism, resist the urge to take it personally. Instead, focus on answering two questions:

1. Putting my personal feelings aside, what can I learn from this alternate perspective?

2. How can I use this feedback to help me improve?

Remember that most criticism is rooted in truth. And even when it isn't, it gives you a valuable window into the perspective of others.

You will begin to see that love and understanding can create a deep sense of wholeness and inner peace. Go out there and bring the passion out, as love always wins.

CHAPTER 6

Face the Fear & Look Outside the Box

Never say never, because limits, like fears, are often just an illusion.
— Michael Jordan

What does it mean to live in "the box"? It's a paradigm, a way of looking at things that give us reasons to stay in our comfort zone. These rationales are mine only and do not necessarily represent the truth. I am used to them, and it is uncomfortable to change, as my in-box brain means my subconscious mind spits out the answers to my conscious awareness. As a result, nothing happens or changes, and we don't find any solution to any problems. When I break the walls of fear and the "box," I can achieve whatever I dream of!

I found out that thinking outside the box is a critical self-leadership and personal development skill that will differentiate between success or failure. Here where most people get stuck!

- I stay in a rut because I am afraid to think outside the box. So many of us stay in unfulfilling jobs or relationships.
- It is the comfort zone that I am so afraid to lose!
- I found through my experience that the meaning of life itself is to create. It's obvious, but when I involve creativity in my relationships, that's not dull.

- Likewise, at work, I need to find new ways to be creative, which leads to better performance in any profession I choose.
- I should be comfortable with creativity and reward it at work. Encourage my team members to think creatively.
- I am open to new ideas and aware that they will add responsibility, discomfort, hard work, and sacrifices. Significant innovations come out of thinking outside the box. I am a leader who must hire and promote rock stars to achieve greatness in business. Everyone can use this forward-thinking in their personal and professional lives. When I was living my life at the ordinary level, I asked myself many questions and, in doing so, came up with more questions.
- I studied and read a lot and found that I could apply the forward-thinking of living out of the box approach to all areas of my life: being at home with my son, in business, in all relationships, in the resentments I held. It requires courage, being a bigger person, and a shift in perception.
- I don't let my fear keep me in the box, keeping a fixed mindset and stealing my dreams and vision for a more fulfilling future. If I wish to get rid of that box mentality and fixed mindset, I will need a positive attitude and to be open to possibilities.
- When I try to achieve my goals or upgrade my mindset and face my fears, I need to write them down — every fear I have — because when I write them down, they are like a mirror, and I reflect on them. I see that most of them are provided by my subconscious mind, so I see that most of them are no longer legitimate.
- I realized that to have a shift in mindset so that I face the fears that paralyze me to take that extra step, it is also essential to have a positive attitude. I feel the fear and do it anyway!

Many people inside the box aren't even aware that they have a negative attitude. Many people have negative self-talk going on, down deep where no one else sees, but they put on a cheerful face to the world, and anger is a fear expressed in public!

ACTION STEPS

- To live outside the box, you must positively destroy the negative image you have about yourself and process the effects of toxic experiences.

- It's our choice how we live our life: a closed or growth mindset! Thinking outside the box is creativity at its finest. That is how some of the most incredible breakthroughs come about.

- Napoleon Hill said, "Whatever the mind of man can conceive and believe, it can achieve." It takes courage and fortitude to believe and heed those words.

- Thinking outside the box creates diversity. It opens new channels of expression and reveals new worlds. Often it makes the channel to what was impossible until now, and in doing so, brings life to a new level. The story of man's progress is the story of thinking outside the box.
- Thinking outside the box is to think differently, unconventionally, or from a new perspective.
- When trying to achieve life goals, your determined mindset will keep you focused on your vision and purpose, no matter how hard the trial is.

Once I opened myself to this possibility, the satisfaction of all aspects of my life has been beyond description. I live my legacy, and that is what I want everyone to experience. Believe me: the beauty of life lies just outside of that box.

Growth Mindset + Positive Habits

Think about and answer the following questions:

1. Name some habits you have now that might be hindering your efforts for success.
2. Write down five habits that could help you reach the success you desire.
3. Have you ever lost a job or damaged a relationship because of bad habits (such as procrastination) that you could not control?
4. Do you believe that any of your present habits interfere with your enjoyment of work, family, or other situations?
5. How would your life be different if you could get rid of some old, harmful habits and replace them with good ones?
6. How do you plan to overcome the obstacles you're sure to face when creating new habits?
7. Explain how you perceive that friends and family will react to your new habits.
8. Think of ways you act around people that are a result of habits you have, either bad or good.
9. Are you taking care of your body so that you are fit and toned? Write down ways to improve your health and fitness and include a plan to reach that goal.
10. Have a plan for how to combat the days when you are tempted to revert to your old habits.
11. Write down some triggers that can sabotage the new habit you are trying to create. Then write down some triggers that might help you keep on track.
12. Name some bad habit triggers and the behavior you exhibit when faced with one of these triggers.

13. What are some rewards that you'll experience from your new habit?
14. Jot down some negative thoughts that always creep into your mind when you try something new and better.
15. Write down some names of people whom you admire and then tell why you admire them.
16. Formulate a plan to learn the necessary skills to achieve success with a new habit.
17. Is the habit you want to abolish or replace linked with an addiction?
18. Jot down some daily changes that will take place in your life with your new habit in place.
19. Is the habit you want to abolish or replace linked with an addiction?
20. Write down some positive things about yourself.

Rome was not built in one day but continued effort and actions and a new powerful habit are not built in one day either. So take the burden for a better you!

Dream it - Envision it - Think it - Grow it - Become it - Live it - Own it.
— Germany Kent

I mastered all these seven (7) steps, so can you too 😊

CHAPTER 7

Ask Yourself & Get the Answers You Need

What you are looking for is not out there...
it's in you.
— Sheryl Sandberg
COO, Facebook

I am amused by human nature! We run through life, looking and searching for satisfaction and fulfillment. We do everything we can to get into the right school, then a good job and career, then finding a good spouse, and then influential friends. We spend to satisfy our ego, buy the most expensive and fashionable dresses, shoes, and handbags to match the shoes. We look for the most expensive homes and furniture, and we look and look and never stop. We are always after something to satisfy ourselves! We look for someone to make us happy: husband, children, friends, coworkers, boss, TV, the list never ends. Often, when things happen in life, we search for answers outside ourselves, asking others for explanations. The cycle never ends. We make the wrong decision, then blame others and complain. We search online to find solutions or satisfaction! At some point, we run out of gas and ask what happened *to* us. But we never recognize that everything happens *through* us! We are the source of everything. It's fascinating that I can stop and be mindful and aware of everything I do or don't do, or say or don't say. Everything I ever need is within me; I have all the answers in the world. I found that using mindfulness meditation allows me to be centered in my experience. If I have any questions, I ask myself and write down everything, and the answer comes organically.

I am the source of everything I experience in my inner world and the outer world. As of now, I know that I make choices from the level of my consciousness. No one can make me happy if I am not able to love myself. No one can help me if I do not help myself. No one can be my friend if I am not my own best friend. No one can hire me if I cannot hire myself. No one will be true to me if I am not loyal to myself. No one will trust me if I do not count on myself.

ACTION STEPS

We are the source; the outer world is our reflection, like a mirror.

- Did you ever look at the bathroom mirror and smile and say to yourself, "I love you"?
- Did you ever look at the bathroom mirror and say to yourself "I forgive you"?
- Did you ever look at the bathroom mirror and say to yourself "I will do it"?

Once you know what this is, you will make better life choices; you won't change your college major several times or keep switching jobs. It's funny that we're usually looking for approval from others, feeling that their approval is more valuable than ours.

- Just be *you* and give love to yourself and every single human on the planet, and you will be the happiest person and live a full life.

- Choose to use empathy, gratitude, and compassion in every interaction with your husband, wife, son, daughter, family,

49

friends, coworkers, boss, competitors, taxi drivers, cleaners, waitresses, supermarket cashiers, doctors, teachers, classmates, banker, accountant, neighbors, and anyone else you encounter.

- Be in a place of peace and ask your inner self. The answer will appear most originally and authentically possible when we allow ourselves that space; we favor ourselves and our community.

- When we only make decisions from our checklist, we often miss the subtle nuances that our intuition brings, and we miss great opportunities.

- No matter what challenges you are facing, you can free yourself from suffering and struggle, and allow yourself to experience life as a mysterious journey of insights. The experience of your senses and inner wisdom is your path to becoming more of who you indeed are and finding inner peace.

- Inner wisdom unlocks the secrets about you, your past, and the events that have shaped you into the person you presently are. Everyone has a story that begins from the moment they are born, but those early chapters do not have to define who you become and who you are at this moment in time.

- Your past experiences have had the most significant impact on your development as a human and spiritual being. These past experiences may be blocking you from fully living life.

- Insights occur when you come to a deeper understanding of the hidden nature of things or perceive some new aspect of yourself — the hidden meanings of things or searching the past for answers to current problems.

- One of the best methods to track your growth is to start a journal. Each day, writing about your experiences in a journal is particularly useful when you have an emotional disturbance like depression or anxiety.

- The best indication that you need to record your thoughts is when you feel a strong negative emotion. Think back to the experience and try to remember what your specific thoughts were. For example, "Now I remember my strong fear of rejection before I opened the door to meet 'him'." These particular thoughts are useful to keep track of because they will help you uncover the core beliefs you operate on.

- The mere act of writing down your thoughts will cause you to bring them into awareness. As a result, you will become more responsive to similar ideas that find their way to the surface of your mind.

In the end, whatever your mind chooses to pursue, make this a conscious choice within you, and choose love, and the love will follow you and everyone around you, as its energy is contagious. And that is formidable!

BE INTIMATE WITH YOUR FEAR

Think of fear as self-sabotage, a misdirected form of self-love. Your brain is moving you toward self-sabotaging behaviors because it thinks that it's protecting you from hurt and danger – when in reality, it's also holding you back from your full potential.

Fear is an emotion most of us prefer to sweep under the rug instead of working to confront head-on. One step you can take to face your inner fears head-on is to journal. Next time you realize that you might be partaking in a self-sabotaging behavior like procrastinating or delaying, take a moment to ask yourself,

"What am I scared of?" and "Why is that scary?" Then ask yourself, "Could I handle it?' Finally, ask yourself, "Does this fear outweigh my desires?" Once you've taken these steps and taken time to consider the situation head-on, the fear inside you loses a little bit of power over your psyche.

- Repeat this activity as needed to train your brain to ease out of old thought patterns slowly.

- Adapt to thrive: you will need to adapt quickly to the culture change, business, or relationship change, and be flexible and resilient.

- Use creativity to become one of the most in-demand skills and cut across many long roads. The invention is always highly prized. Distill it into your daily strategy.

- Develop emotional intelligence: collaboration and active listening — making a conscious effort to concentrate on what is said and focusing on the speaker's body language and other cues — will become more valuable. People who have expertise in interpersonal skills and empathy will be in demand in a transforming workplace.

- Coaching and mentoring will also become a core part of managing changing teams effectively. Employers are looking for high emotional intelligence — the ability to communicate and collaborate.

- Everyone wants to be treated kindly; it seems like a no-brainer, but often when we speak about leadership, treating people kindly is overlooked.
  Being kind contributes to making others happy. Happiness makes people about 12 percent more productive.

- Here are some reasons leaders should focus on kindness rather than just being nice and some tips on doing so.

- Kind actions are praised and remembered: they have a 'boomerang' effect.

- Kindness and other such acts cost nothing to give but create significant value.

As a leader, kindness leads to you not only being thought of fondly but also helps your bottom line by cultivating a positive work culture. How can you incorporate kindness?

Try doing a kind act in your tribe every day for two weeks and see how you feel.

Try to think of acts of kindness to yourself as well. Haven't those made a difference to you?

- Showing empathy when dealing with situations.

- Forgiving mistakes that are made on the job.

- Finally, showing your appreciation and thanks to everyone.

CHAPTER 8

Giving & Receiving is Healing

Practice random acts of kindness and senseless acts of beauty.
— Jack Canfield

Giving and receiving is one of the most fundamental gifts that God gives to humans. It's a powerful way of expressing love, appreciation, caring, sharing, and helping in the most profound way to express your feelings of togetherness and sense of belonging. Since the beginning of time, we are wired to share; from the moment a baby is born, the mother gives love and her own life to the baby. When everything is frozen in cold of winter, the father finds food and shares the last piece with his child or neighbor. In hot desert lands, people share the last drop of water so everyone survives. Today, we share care, service, knowledge, and undivided attention of love and understanding. It's the universal law that in modern days we call the law of attraction. When you feel low, or something terrible happens, you lean on your loved one, pull yourself together, and get up again, and you indeed will find love. And from there, start over again by giving and receiving. There is a big heart racing and passionately trying to express the gratitude and love behind every gift we receive, like a smile, a helping hand, a book, a coffee cup, and the PPP grant the government gives to help the small businesses. It is a beautiful thing to be a human and experience these feelings that fill your heart most deeply and undoubtedly that comes from heaven. I am fortunate to experience both giving and receiving, and my heart is so full of love and appreciation that I want to share it with everyone.

EXAMPLE

I open the mail, and I see a package. I look at the address to see if it's for me and who could have sent it. It is for me!
I open it; it is from Lizzy at Smith College! I couldn't believe that; this is a gift for me. I open and see inside the most precious and thoughtful gift that my beautiful friends sent me! It's a small, exquisite, light-green-colored self-care purse with a zipper, and everything inside is well-designed: the same-colored face-cleaning sponge, nail polish, small jar of hand cream, mouth mints, and a beautify pen along with a journal from Smith College!

My heart is racing, and my eyes are shining from happy tears. What a fantastic feeling; it's priceless. It's bigger than life! What a quality, meaningful, and profound effect has on human life is a blessing on earth.

All my life, I have this feeling that I want to help as many people as I can with everything I have or do. I started feeling this way when I was nine years old, and I continued with it all my life. Giving is medicine for the soul and makes people smile. That is the biggest reason I will continue with this journey as long as I can. To make someone smile is my duty in life as I live in a state of gratitude all my life.

- Sometimes, when you're going through tough times, you can use giving to others as a way to heal yourself and come back from burnout or setbacks. As we all know, the good and the harmful spectrums never end. So, look around, choose love, and care, as that is the medicine for our soul.

- When you feel low or think of yourself as a victim (which we are the authors of in our own lives), visit a hospital and see how lucky you are. Go and visit St. Jude Children's Hospital rather than ruminating on all the wrong things with your day; focus on what went right. By giving your time, your service, or your meal, your money, or your smile, or anything, you will feel alive and useful. As a human, you can make a difference in someone's life, and by doing that, you heal your soul in the process.

- We are spiritual beings in a human body. Therefore, it is critical to maintain all parts of ourselves—our mind, body, and spirit. We are simple, but at the same time very complicated, and on top of that, we complicate things ourselves. Try to control your mind, and not let your mind control you!

- Be aware of the energy that you send out; the law of gravity says that what you send out comes back to you. Give love as it bounces back to you!

- Practice giving everywhere you go and to every person you meet.

- Give love, care, smiles, time, money, food, your home, jobs, hugs, massages, knowledge, attention, understanding, compassion, blood, forgiveness, gratitude, helping hands, your shoulder, and your life to the love.

- Emit love, and care as we are all humans no matter what race or color we are. It's the gift for which God put us on this earth.

EXAMPLE

"Desi, you have so much to do. May I help you?" asked Katya. "Oh, no, thank you, I am OK." "Okay then, see you tomorrow,"

Katya answered as she closed the office door behind her. I know that I had so much to do, but I believed that no one could do the job in the same way I do. So, I worked hard and refused to accept help, so I burned the candle at both ends!

Is this the right way to handle the job?

Is this a limiting belief? Yes, it is.

If I thought out of the box, I could accept the help or delegate the job to other coworkers and train and include my colleagues in the process. Perhaps they wouldn't do the tasks exactly as I did them, but they would learn if I could share.

How will people understand if you don't share and teach?

Teach your colleagues so that you won't burn out in the future, and they will help you get your work done. Everyone will be involved and working as a team.

As odd as it may seem, people feel uncomfortable when others give to them all the time and they fail to give anything back. The thing is, giving back happens in an infinite number of ways. The person who receives can give something different to someone else to continue the give-and-receive cycle. The chances are high that the receiver will not give anything back to the giver but will provide something of equal or more excellent value to another person or project.

- It's the fundamentals of applying the **beautiful law of giving and receiving that we do that is the law of attraction that** we follow, and everything is in harmony.

- Don't fall into the mental trap of harmful assumptions. It's easy to spiral out of control.

- It's natural to try to analyze and assess people and situations to make sense of our surroundings. The danger lies in allowing your imagination to wander too far, leading to the 'worst-case-scenario,' which causes anxiety, frustration, and fear.

- Furthermore, the assumptions you make about how people feel about you or say to you are often reflections of how you feel about yourself.

- If you're feeling ignored, alone, or abused and your first thought is,

'They treat me this way because _____,' or

'They must think that I'm _____,'

then what you're doing is projecting your feelings about yourself. If this behavior goes unchecked and you don't realize that you're making silly assumptions, you will trick your mind into making false judgments about other people.

CHAPTER 9

The Beauty of Cleaning Out Old Chips in Your Brain

Rephrase, Renew, Rebuild

The symbolic language of the crucifixion is the death of the old paradigm. Resurrection is a leap into a whole new way of thinking.
— Deepak Chopra

When our cars get old, we take them to the mechanic to change parts to work well again! When something happens with computer chips, we change them. When we add files to our computer, they are there when we need them. It's what happens with our brain; whatever we store there, it's available for our use! To update our mindset and be aware of our (files') limitations, to compare our perception to reality, we must be mindful to choose what files (thoughts) we put in our brain that can be crucial to how we live our lives. Perhaps this is not a sophisticated way to describe what happens, but it is efficient! It affects our lives most profoundly. In this case, to update and delete my old and infected thoughts that do not serve but instead destroy me, and replace them with powerful and positive forward-thinking, is the best favor I can do for myself, my community, and my loved ones. In that way, we thrive as a family, organization, or in any relationship.

Here is what I discovered:

I met Bill in our Meetup networking meeting in a very cozy local restaurant in our area. We introduced each other, and we engaged in all sorts of conversations, business, professional, and personal, and as we enjoyed drinking our rosé, the conversation took off. As he explained his business, his insights were useful. He had a cheerful, intelligent, and friendly personality, and immediately, one understood that he worked in sales and the financial world. He continued his conversation with his pleasant attitude as he explained his business. When he started to speak about his relationship with his spouse, his voice changed. He said, "! could not take her any longer… she is too much; she spent irresponsibly, and does not do or get anything I say. We both just could not see things the same anymore…we are arguing all the time!"

I certainly understood his longing and discontent, that he was thinking that there was something better out there, as his voice cracked; and I understood that unconsciously he was looking for an answer.

As a coach and consultant, working for a very long time with people at many levels in their lives and stages of development, I asked: "How long has it been like that?"

"About one year!" he replied.

"And how many years have you been married?"

"For about seventeen years."

"What is your part in creating or allowing this to happen?"

"Well, I want her to stop doing what she is doing, and yes, I am bored."

"What would you love to happen here? What steps would you take, and what request would you make to get what you want?" I added.

He stopped speaking and got deep into his thoughts. His facial expression changed, and he was uncomfortable.

No one spoke. I let it be!

Then he continued: "This is a long story, as we are on a networking event, but can I call you tomorrow at 2:00 p.m.? I really would like to hear your advice."

"Certainly. Let me see my calendar." I checked the calendar on my phone. "Yes, I am available to meet you tomorrow at 2:00 p.m." Then I went on.

"Bill, what would it be like if just for a moment you allowed yourself to imagine a different possibility to happen here, and if you wrote down other areas in your life that are bothersome? It would be a great way to reflect on what's been happening. In the next step, you will ask your wife how she sees you, so we could evaluate and have clarity on what needs to be done, okay? And we can discuss it when we meet in our session tomorrow."

"Wow, this never crossed my mind to do; this is a great approach. I am eagerly waiting to discover and share with you tomorrow."

"Great, looking forward to meeting you tomorrow. Don't forget to bring a notebook along with you."

"Yes indeed."

We shake hands and say goodbye!

That was an on-the-spot coaching session with Bill, in which I offered help to this almost burnt-out, on-the-verge-of divorce executive. The rest is history!

In a typical case of limitations and habits, one must be willing to be open to the possibility of seeing one's limiting beliefs and the downside of staying in the world of blame and complaints. Get out of that world and evaluate your emotions and motives and the other person. We all live in a paradigm that is often untrue, and every story has two sides. Make the time to get to know your partner better, and you may discover that there are many more reasons to love him or her than previously believed.

ACTION STEPS

It's a beautiful Tuesday morning as I go through the paperwork to prepare the folder of one of our faculty members to promote him to the next stage of his career. Suddenly, at the office door, John, a junior executive, showed up. "Hello, John, how are you this morning?" I asked.

"I am so upset with that idiot woman that I hired... I made a big mistake—I should not have hired her! She is giving me such an attitude. I just can't take it any longer. How can I get her out?" he asked, and from the nuance of his voice, I felt his worries and anger.

"How come? You pushed so hard to hire her in record time as you valued her so much! What is your part in creating or allowing this to happen?" It was the third time within the same week that he was coming back to complain about the same thing! I gave him tips to use to smooth the relationship, but he was just resisting his responsibility. It took me a long time to coach and cool him down to see the light, be open and be coachable.

Many executives go through the same issues every day!

Do you think that your employee gives you a bad attitude and his/her productivity is suffering?

How long have these challenges been going on?

- What are the most important and frequent activities?
- What behavioral style and temperament are most naturally suited to do this type of work?
- How quickly will the successful individual need to learn new information and skills?
- How flexible and adaptable will the person need to be in this role?
- What specific knowledge, skills, and abilities are required?

When you are about to hire someone, follow these datapoints:

Knowledge • Skills • Education • Behavioral profile • Cognitive ability • Values

- You can collect this additional information through behavioral, cognitive, skills, or values assessments administered after the initial screening.
- Understand how a candidate compares to existing team members. Taking a talent optimization approach to hiring means taking a data-driven look at candidates and considering how you match the available role, the existing team, and the organization's culture.
- Is the candidate wired to behave the same as the rest of the team? Or is there something about their personality that might clash with others on the team?

Looking deep in yourself and seeing what is missing and evaluating your core values and vision by being vulnerable enough and sharing with your team will make all the difference. Their behavior reflects your behavior and attitude. Perhaps look back and see the patterns of similar situations so that you can be aware of your limitations.

Great leaders use this powerful formula every day: Event plus Your Response equals the Outcome you get! As with every experience in your life, success or failure, sickness or joy, and wealth or poverty result from how you respond to early events or events in real-time.

- When was the last time you asked for feedback from your team?

Asking for feedback is a powerful tool to use to your advantage to grow and prosper as a leader. Find the reason why they act the way they do. The team, spouse, child feedback is telling you that you are off course. To get back on time, you need to appreciate that feedback which requires the leader to take appropriate action, keep open communication lines, and act like you are the right leader! Create a safe space and ask them how they see you as limiting yourself for the team, how and what it will take to improve everyone's performance to get back on course. It will be better for everyone, better for the teams, and better for running the business.

- What impact are these challenges having in other areas of your life?

Look at all areas of your life and find patterns that you will need to disrupt and replace with empowering habits and attitudes. Stretch to educate yourself and search for any limitations; you will see the difference in how you see things and events so that you can act for the greater good.

- Are you a good listener?

Ask most people if they're a good listener, and they'll say, 'of course!' But very few of us are good at listening effectively.

A study of over 8,000 employees from various job backgrounds found that almost all participants believed they communicated effectively or more effectively than their coworkers. The average person listens at only about 25% efficiency! While most people agree that listening is an essential skill, most don't feel a strong need to improve that skill.

A study of managers and employees in a high-stress hospital setting found that listening explained 40% of ineffective leadership variance.

- Think of someone you believe to be an effective leader in your life – be it a teacher, a politician, a boss, or even a parent. Would you consider them to be a good listener?
- As a leader, working on your listening skills will foster bonds and trust between yourself and your subordinates.
- Like I mentioned before, humans are social creatures who thrive on relationships; this means that one of the BEST things you can do for another person is to show them that their communication is working and that their message is delivered effectively.
- Think of a time that you sat down with someone, discussed your thoughts in a way that almost left you with a sense of relief when you walked away.

While you might be thinking that your multitasking skills are good enough to hold a conversation while simultaneously doing something else, no doubt making a habit will create some tension between you and your conversing partners. If your goal is to better connect with someone, you should be making an effort to work WITH them instead of telling them what to do. As an active listener, your ultimate goal is to get as much information as possible in a time-efficient manner and leave the conversation on better terms and achieve high performance.

What I see starts with *me*. — Mary Morrissey

CHAPTER 10

How to Live on Fire Without Burning Out

Successful and unsuccessful people do not vary greatly in their abilities. They vary in their desires to reach their potential.
— John C. Maxwell

Life! The most precious gift that God gives *us*! Are we fully aware of what we do with it? The chances are that most of the time, we are not. At some point, I have asked myself: Who and where am I, and what am I doing?

This question comes for everyone at different periods in their life, and for me, it came when I turned forty.

We strive to find meaning within ourselves and find our place in the family, school, career, and society. We try hard to find our home because, as mammals, we try to adapt, and we want to be liked and accepted. We hardly ask ourselves who we are! Everyone is born with his or her unique gift or talent. It is within our control as to whether we commit to finding out what we are passionate about, or we simply go through the motions of life. We live in that paradigm without knowing what our real calling is!

- I found that out by following my passion and doing what I love, I am aware most of the time and feel like I'm losing track of time when I am doing what I love! It's a fantastic feeling!

- When I do what I love, I feel energized and satisfied, even in challenging situations, as I align with my core values and purpose.

- Even in the middle of uncertainty or failure—which for me are not failures—these are stepping-stones to finding a better solution and never tiring in trying a better way that I am passionate about.

- The outcome will be outstanding. After all, I can develop solutions that I never dreamt about because I am passionate and in total harmony with myself, my family, my coworkers, and my community.

- My satisfaction level is high, productivity is high, and the impact in my community is high. As the fire inside me never dies, so it is when I am aware and using my fire. "The world is not enough," the famous James Bond said in a movie, implying that by aligning with my mind, body, and spirit, I operate at my higher self and, as a result, I strive for outstanding results for my community and society at large.

- As a high achiever, I work and do everything with passion, and I put my heart, spirit, and mind into everything I do. I strive for perfection, which does not exist!

- Whether I work for one person or three people, it doesn't matter because anything is possible for me. I say *yes* to almost everything and anyone! I never give up chasing achievements because I want to be inspiring and do good for my community. Nothing is impossible, and I work more than the rest of the team. I motivate and engage people and help them to gain more knowledge.

- I feel satisfied and take pride when I make a difference in other people's lives because I know I can make a difference for the better in anything I do. My passion never leaves me; it is like a forever train trip!

- My vision is more significant than me, and sometimes freezes me until I get used to it! I put my time, courage, soul, money, unwavering dedication, faith, and knowledge into something I believe will positively impact my community, family, or loved ones! I take any setback, missteps, or other people's shortcomings and limitations, and I turn them into uplifting and unstoppable, inspiring action and successful results.

Most achievers I know are people who have made a strong and deep dedication to pursue a goal. That dedication took a tremendous amount of effort.
— Donald Johanson

EXAMPLE

Exploring the unknown, and enjoying every bit of it, is a must, even we know that life has twists, turns, and is often unpredictable and challenging. But high achievers gracefully overcome the unexpected.

That happens over and over again in my life!

It's a beautiful Tuesday morning, and I walked into my office at City Hall. I met with my staff for their updates and greeted everyone in the hallway. There were many projects underway, and many decisions were required. I went through my folders and decided to create a committee to organize and oversee the European Union operations, which had provided humanity aid for Albania since the country had just emerged from Communist rule. Poverty and pain were rampant among the Albanian people. Some people wanted to take advantage of themselves and their "ego" rather than thinking of hundreds of thousands of people suffering.

I called upon the staff members, and as a team, we developed the strategy and procedures and used all the warehouses to distribute goods to every family in the city and surrounding towns.

Hard work is required, but the satisfaction of knowing that every family received food, clothing, and goods is worth every minute, day, and night of hard work and nights without sleep, and tirelessly taking care to the very littlest details. None of us had any field experience from our experience living in a communist country. The only thing I had was my passion, compassion, mission, and persistence, and with the help of my faithful friends, I wanted every household to have food and smiles. I overcame every obstacle that I encountered, and I never gave up following my calling to help and be of service. I am just 26 years old. The same thing happened when the community decided to build housing for the people who no longer would be squeezed into small apartments, as was the norm under the communist regime. Despite some roadblocks and people who were trying to take advantage of the situation, I organized a City Hall committee to proactively develop a policy and procedures to ensure that immediate needs were met of those who suffered and were in extreme conditions from the regime. The road for the greater good is not always easy, but the power of persistence and the desire to see everyone happier gave me courage. The firm will and the fire within; that is what we need to keep alive to see the bigger picture, why high achievers do not dare but carry on and find ways to put people together, so everyone prospers and lives the lives they love. I engage people in conversation, educate, and understand the process.

Stretching yourself beyond your limits and exploring the unknown to deliver profound value to your people and society should always be pursued as a Greater Purpose.

ACTION STEPS

The downside to being high achievers is that we take on more than we can handle for an extended period. We're workaholics because we put our hearts and passions into everything, and we're usually Type A personalities. We tend not to delegate as we strive for excellence, and we think that we are the only ones who can do the job in the way we do it.

- We tend to overlook other areas of our lives until we reach the burnout point. Making things worse is that we could have upgraded our mindset, perception, and flexibility regularly by being inclusive, delegating, training, and involving everyone on the team or family.

- We need to synchronize our mind, body, and heart to bring balance.

- We need to be mindful in our thinking, perception, communication, and behavior as all our results will depend on these.

- We need to be mindful of any feedback we receive at any given moment and take that as a mirror to reflect so we can see our actions' results.

- There is no such thing as the perfect work-life balance. Given the many demands made on everyone today, you need to be mindful and strive for simplicity, and be priority-based in all aspects of your life.

- You need to remind yourself to "get back to basics." Synchronize what is not in alignment. For me and millions of others, practicing meditation and maintaining a healthy lifestyle is essential to get my fires burning. As we know, everyone does best when operating from the level of their consciousness.

- Our brain is like a computer chip, and what we put there gets stored. Like a computer, we need time to check and delete the old files that do not serve us any longer and upgrade with new ones. Everything depends on what files of our brain we use at any given moment.

Let's use the following formula:

- What are two things you can do daily to feed your mind?
- What are two things you can read in the next 90 days?
- What are two things you can do daily to feed your body?
- What are your ultimate goals and aspirations for this year?
- Is there something you would like to learn from a "role model" over the next 90 days?
- List a handful of people who could be perfect fits to be the right "role model "for you.
- What are the ideal characteristics of your perfect proximity? What do they like, dislike, support you with?

- What are some action steps you can take in the next two weeks to find the perfect "proximity" in your life?
- What are some massive action steps you can take over the next 90 days?
- What are three ways you can give back to someone in need in the next 30 days?
- What are the self-giving consequences you will receive if you don't accomplish your goals?
- What would your dream life look like if you finally achieved your most important goals? Write it in detail.
- Write down 1-3 times when you let your emotions get the best of you, and you were angry, enraged, depressed, etc.
- Write down what *emotions/actions* you could have *had/taken* instead of those negative emotions.
- Make a list of lousy words you find yourself using that you think could trigger negative emotions.
- How many people do you know who know what to do but don't do what they know? Decide upfront why you're doing this.

Use Rational Decision-Making

- Articulate and define the problem.
- Identify and weigh each criterion value.
- Provide a common metric for comparing.
- Identify alternatives.
- Rate each alternative along with the criteria.
- Compute scores and select the highest.

Adapt to thrive in this gig economy; more organizations will hedge their bets on hiring workers that will need to adapt quickly to a company's culture and be flexible and resilient.

PART II

EVERYTHING WE NEED IS INSIDE US!

Persistence is probably the single most common quality

longer you hang in there, the greater the chance that something will happen in your favor. No matter how hard it seems, the longer you persist the more likely your success.
— Jack Canfield

CHAPTER 11

Be Persistent & Satisfied

Abraham Lincoln! There is probably no better example of failure and persistence that I know of.

When you're on a mission to make a difference in people's lives, go beyond the apparent limits, and explore unknown territory to find out what would be possible. When conditions are rigid, you go on against the odds. Deep inside us is that burning fire that lets us know there is a solution to everything that appears. It's the sense of knowing that goodness will be revealed, no matter what! It's an unspoken law that God added to the earth and that the good, the bad, and the ugly existed from the beginning of time, and that is the beauty of life itself. Imagine if only the *good* existed—we wouldn't be able to distinguish anything. That would be very boring, and perhaps that's the reason the mix exists on our planet Earth, and that is extraordinary!

For high achievers, it is essential to see the big picture in any given situation. Doing that provides a sense of knowing what to do. Persistence comes organically and is part of high achievers' traits. Agility distinguishes extraordinary thinking, being, and living from ordinary thought, being, and living! It's hard for an ordinary person to handle and take the burden when the world falls in front of their eyes. Still, a person who possesses persistence knows that there is always another way to solve any given problem. By saying *no*, some of us don't make any difference. By not finding the solution for the problem at hand, some do not make a difference. What makes a difference is a persistence that a person possesses, which means he or she will never stop searching for a better solution that aligns with the universe's law.

It happened when my mentor, Jack Canfield, was rejected 143 times but never gave up his vision and mission until he got the *"yes"* on the 144th time for his *Chicken Soup for the Soul* book series that now has reached millions of readers! That is the extraordinary power of persistence! It happened when I got burned out and failed as a professional and person from my limiting beliefs, mindset, and habits that cost me to live the job I loved! I divorced, got sick, almost died in the hospital, sold my home, and took out my retirement money to pay for my business expenses. Everyone was freaking out and telling me that I should not follow my dream to become a consultant and a coach. I never gave up on my vision, my faith, and my friends' support! Now I am a delighted person and a successful businesswoman! My passion is for helping as many people as possible and bringing abundance to as many people as possible.

It happened when I went from being an attorney to a position in the law office at the Tirana City Hall in Albania's capital. With my passion for helping as many people as possible and bringing abundance to as many people as possible, I was well aware of how much these people, including myself, were suffering—it was my burning desire, persistence, and determination that I brought to the cause.

As you might imagine, after one country with big problems went from communist totalitarianism to democracy, it was a fragile time with people thirsty for freedom and prosperity after suffering so much under communism. I worked to help put in place new procedures to switch from "no one's government" to a democratic government! With no experience of what democracy meant I started to apply the European Union laws for internal and external affairs and put policies and procedures for the local and central government. It was a very volatile time and not easy, as people were familiar with the old practices that had not been working for themselves for forty-seven years. Every day there were meetings to discuss and apply a new process for the policies. I studied day and night to help implement the new democratic system at the Tirana City Hall law office. I learned case after case and brainstormed with the office director to make the necessary changes as we went along. I collaborated with Bari and Rome City Hall offices in Italy for possible assistance. I was among four lawyers and the director at the Tirana City Hall law office. Still, you could count on only two, and the director who worked like the other two members knew nothing about law and had no desire to learn. Jean and I handled all city legal issues and worked nonstop to manage the tremendous demands and workload. Computers were arriving from the European Union. As one could imagine, after the end of communism, the office became a classroom after the workday, with people pouring into the office asking for help for a million different issues. The need to service the citizens was at the center of the work for me and many others who delivered the burning desires, longings and millions of dreams of thirsty people. That is where leadership, passion, persistence, and determination met, and without these qualities, we could not achieve greatness and serve a greater good. We proudly fulfilled what we were entrusted to do for the city and the country.

ACTION STEPS

Developing the power of persistence in any business or enterprise looks at the following steps that may help you prosper.

- Avoid comparison with others.
- Be prepared to adjust your approach or strategy.
- Keep your vision and mission in mind.
- Upgrade always the right attitude to keep motivation up.
- Seek support, as no one stands alone.
- Upgrade processes that no longer work.
- See and feel the approach.
- Create a sense of urgency.
- Be a role model.
- Measure and approach resistance.
- Get insightful about any project.
- Identify the resistance points and find solutions.
- Measure the outcome.
- Find a grounding approach.

Be the one to pursue and possess these qualities, and you will undoubtedly prevail.

Persistence in Positive Growth Habits

The more you can learn and understand how you and your team members operate, the more productive all can become. These questions can help you work with them to understand their work habits and help them build them.

- What part of the day do you have the most energy and focus? When do you have the least?
- What changes could be made to your work schedule to accommodate this?
- What is a perfect, productive day at work for you? Please walk me through the day.
- What's an inexpensive thing that can be done to improve your office environment?
- What are the biggest time-wasters for you each week?
- What makes you excited and motivated to work on a project?

- When you get stuck on something, what is your process for getting unstuck? Who do you turn to for help?
- What part of your work routine do you find is working best? What area do you want to improve?
- What do you do when you feel low-energy or unmotivated?
- How can I help you?

Be the one to pursue and possess these qualities, and you will undoubtedly prevail.

CHAPTER 12

How to Follow Your Dream and Your Inner Genius

You do not become what you want; you become what you believe.
— Oprah Winfrey

There was a girl with a Big Dream.
Love in her heart that everyone could see.
She went up and down but never stopped.
Chasing her dream from the inside out!
One can ask: How could she be real?
And the girl smiles, as she knows that is real!
— Desi Tahiraj

Living life by pursuing your dreams is the most fulfilling way to live. There is simply no comparison. When we are young, we have big dreams, but we forget about them as we go through life with its ups and down! We go through our survival mode and our life is monotonous, and we ignore them or become afraid to pursue them. We trade our true happiness for our mediocre security! Imagine if *every one* of us pursues our dreams that we hold so dear and we become free of the limitations that stop us from doing so. The world would undoubtedly be a better place to live. When we are satisfied and everyone around us is also content, when businesses thrive and everyone does what they love, harmony and happiness are present. I had a dream that kept me up at night and did not give up on me!

Do you ever feel that everywhere you go, and every time you think of your dream or goal, it makes you smile just considering it? You feel energized, happy, and inspired to overcome anything that stands in the way. No matter what might stop you, you try again and again and never give up! That is what I did about my dream and not giving up on my pursuit!

EXAMPLE

Government offices are filled with people asking for help with their requests and demands for quick results. I was on a mission to help as many as I could. Every morning at the law office in City Hall, the director and the four attorneys there met to split the tremendous number of cases that needed to be resolved. I took a big briefcase with ten court cases, mostly citizen-to-citizen property and relationships disputes, which were the significant Albanian issues, especially in the capital city. At eight o'clock, City Hall opened to take requests from the citizens. A lovely elderly couple entered the office. "How can I help you?" "Hi, ma'am. We are tired of going from office to office, and no one is helping us!" the man said with a quivering voice. I could hear the pain, longing, and discontent in this his voice. "We would like to ask for your help as it has been a year since I was kicked out of my photo shop and painting studio and home on the second floor. My grandfather, father, and I own it, but someone made false documents, registered it in his name, and took me to the police and registration office to kick me out. The police came to my shop to kick me out of my shop!"

He explained his problem and had trouble getting his words out. He was soft-spoken, confused, and anxious. His wife kept quiet; tears were streaming down her cheeks, and her lips were quivering. The purse in her hand was shaking from her hands' uncontrolled movement. "Show me your property documents," I replied. Ilia, the man, passed the documents to me. I took a few minutes to go through them, took a deep breath, explained the procedure to them, and then stated: "These are the originals, and I needed copies to investigate the case." "I'll go right now to make a copy if you wish," said Ilia. "No need to go out and spend money." I sent him to the administrative assistant to get two copies made. Ilia came back soon after with a glimmer of hope in his eyes! I kept the copies of the documents and explained to Ilia and his wife that they would need to follow court procedures, and they eventually ended up opening a court case. I nodded as this type of situation was common in Albania at that time and continues to this day, with sometimes three different people claiming to be the owner of the same property. I promised the couple that I would help to resolve the situation, but I didn't know how much time it would take at that point as I needed to investigate. The couple looked at ease and surprised because they had been to three different offices to complain, but no one had offered to take up the case! For sure!

It was the morning of October 4th and I woke up early to prepare for court. That day was the final session, as the case had gone back and forth between the local and appeals court after I had shown the last original documents that proved the legitimacy of ownership for the family for over three generations. It had taken a long time and lots of effort, searching for clues and getting pictures of the property over the years in different offices. Ilia and his wife lost hope, and they arrived in despair. However, I never lost hope. We meet with Ilia and his wife at the court's main door. The opponent and his lawyer stopped in front of me, and with anger, said, "We have everything in our hands, and we will get the property guaranty." "Sir, I understand your frustration as this is taking so long! I represent City Hall, and we follow our legal procedures, and the property has been in the Ilia family name for three generations. If you bring to court the documents that overthrow the ownership, I will be glad to back off." His lawyer took the client to the side and stopped him from saying anything else, and apologized. Ilia appeared at the courtroom door...in his face, I saw his desperation and fear. "I know we are not going to win the case. We couldn't sleep all night," he whispered. "Not to worry, it will be just fine," I said, smiling, as I already had in my head and my folder the solution!

The session began, and I did something that no one did in court at that time. I gave a copy of the documents to the judge and one to the opponent. I explained that she had original documents from four different offices. The opponent had registered on June 14th of this year to the archives and property registration office. And it was clear that the description didn't match the story of the property. The report was of another property. On the other document, someone had written over the old information.

I took out a magnifying glass to show the judge the documents. There was dead silence, and then the man said, "This is impossible, no ma'am, this is impossible."

The man didn't know that I had gone and searched in many places, asked many friends to find the originals and back-up documents, and I had not said a word to Ilia and his wife for the sake of conspiracy! The judge and two of the other members of the jury examined the documents. The judge then announced the case had to resume now, and we were to come back in three hours with the verdict. Ilia and his wife were in disbelief over what just happened! For the first time in almost two years, they were smiling! They tried to offer me lunch. I thanked them and said I had to go back to my office to use those three hours to prepare for another dispute the next day in court that was between City Hall and a citizen being charged with fraud. I went back to court to hear the verdict—and indeed, as I had foreseen, it was in favor of Ilia and his family. The family was the legitimate owner of the photo/painting shop. Ilia and his wife began crying out of happiness, and they couldn't stop thanking and hugging me. It was a unique feeling of fulfillment for all of them and for me, as I fulfilled God's request to help as many people as possible that I could. (This is for another book, as I have a special relationship with God, and it is my job to be of service.) 😊

Natural leaders rise even in the most unlikely of places and times! Growth and rebirth are part of life.

ACTION STEPS

Follow your dream no matter how hard it is, as your dream's fulfillment is the most beautiful feeling. What you become in the process is extraordinary! Time tests us all, as it's part of life, but don't you dare to give up! We can experience ups and downs, but don't let setbacks define our life; Instead, use them to continue to develop as a person and leader.

Don't let the circumstances define your life. Chasing your dream and growing with it will provide the most satisfaction that anyone can experience, and when it is time to look back and see what your life was about, you will be glad you did, as it's better to risk it than to regret it!

Go out there and be *you*, with a big heart, big vision, and wisdom

- Encourage Debate.

- Emphasize Empathy.

- Encourage Laughter.

- Build bridges; think we, not me.

- Establish a baseline of owed respect.

- Recognize that respect has ripple effects.

- Know when efforts to convey respect can backfire.

- Create a list of a fun list that your team loves that you will engage weekly.

- Create accountability, feedback, and peer coaching as part of your culture.

Ask employees regular feedback questions is an agile and lightweight way of keeping up with what's going on. Answers become conversations about what is essential and meaningful for the team and the company, and those conversations transform into action.

1. What's going well in your role? Any wins this week? It is a great place to start as you get to celebrate and even brag a little about all the positive stuff that happened during the week by simply answering that question.

2. What challenges are you facing? Where are you stuck? The quickest way to overcome challenges and get unstuck is to say, "I'm stuck!" When we can identify the workplace problems and then bring someone else's attention to the challenge at hand, we can receive the coaching and guidance that helps us think about the issue in a fresh new way. Often just writing about where we're stuck begins the process of clarifying how to resolve it ourselves.

3. What is the business doing, or can it be doing, to make you more successful? You don't know what you don't know until you ask the right question.

4. How are you feeling? What's the morale around you? Asking how you feel is critical. It increases motivation and happiness because collective experiences feel validated and heard.

The answers to this feedback question can also allow you to correctly time-specific initiatives and changes within yourself and the company.

Are you or your team on the edge of burnout or feeling happy and energized?

Are you stressed about the new product launch?

5. On a scale of 1-10, how happy are you? Why?

Satisfaction is a precursor to success and accomplishment, not the other way around. When you and your team are happy, you not only come up with better solutions, but their satisfaction also helps to build organizational culture. By quantifying happiness, you can emit high performance.

6. What's the best thing that happened to you this week, either at work or outside of it?

It can help you develop more commitment and engagement. Feeling that others know and understand your desires and goals helps maintain high team productivity. Throw out ideas for improvement, no matter how big or how small. What's one thing you would do differently?

You can also develop an internal conversation regarding improvements and better ask this question to elicit specific and constructive feedback on how to be a better leader.
Ask your associates who know you best and who can give you honest insights and feedback. Success is the result of aligning your vibe to your tribe. Ask for feedback or constructive criticism. Evaluate, test, perfect your actions, do the hard work, learn from failure, and stay loyal and persist as greatness begins beyond our comfort zone.

CHAPTER 13

Relating & Adapting – How to Win with the Determination of Your Soul

---

Put your heart, mind, intellect, and soul even to your smallest acts. This is the secret of success.
— Swami Sivananda

We all use determination unconsciously in our day-to-day activities, but we rarely make a conscious choice to use it in things that matter most to us. We get wrapped up in small things, then one day, we regret that we did not go after our dream. We regret that we did not put time and effort into something and the activities we love the most. When that happens, we live in a state of disappointment.

As a driven person, I found that I put love in everything I do, and the passion and determination come naturally to me. Often, I see people give up on things they love when they find out that the work is too hard or complicated. That is just a mindset that keeps us wedded to the familiar and doesn't allow the beauty to prevail.

Also, everyone would agree that the sense of belonging and feeling loved is the beauty of humans. We need to understand the importance of building up a strong foundation, the inner peace of success, belonging, and Tribe. From there, we see how life is, to build layer upon layer, one step at a time in any business. We live in a volatile, multicultural world, and each of us brings in different cultures, languages, and circumstances. Therefore, it is easy to see why it is essential to look at what we have the same and leverage the differences. Within us, we have everything, good and bad, and we choose the good by what we are and how we build our tribe. Influential leaders understand and manage the underlying psychology of employees' responses to the change and clarify decision-making. To gain clarity in your decision-making you first need to monitor your moods. How you handle ambiguous and stressful situations, how we are perceived by and interact with others, and reflect that to your employees. Know your irritability trigger that struggles with pride and others' expectations so you can manage your reactions. So, when you face real business challenges, you won't find it difficult to admit you need help. Realize that you don't need to do everything yourself. Clarify and communicate that every single employee at every level has a role to play in that change. Whether you're fully aware of the problem and need help solving it; know how to solve it but need validation; or know there's a problem but can't pinpoint it exactly, you likely already know bad news is on its way. It's even worse when they discover they needed more help than you thought.

Most importantly, communicating early and often, no matter how large or small the change, can mean the difference between success and failure in adopting change. The more the message resonates, the more likely employees are to feel valued. When communication is clear, employees feel valued, and everyone feels they have a role to play, and the smooth adoption of change is inevitable.

Spread love – be people-oriented, which is the foundation of life and prosperity that grows our strengths, retains the power within, and builds self-esteem, faith, passion, and enthusiasm. Every employee is triggered to innovate and create processes and solutions that serve all and bring happiness and contentment. Inject resilience so all your company will adapt to life's changes and crises and therefore build character, commitment, courage, and confidence.

An intelligent person would see that self-awareness decreases stress, improves attention span, and reduces job burnout, and any external pain that stresses you is not due to the thing itself but to your own interpretation of it. And this you have the power to revoke at any moment.

EXAMPLE

It was Friday evening in November 2018. I was pleased to receive a Certification Award from Navara Business School for my Leadership Development Program and Doing Business Globally. I felt satisfied that all my hard work and determination had allowed me to complete this degree. At the same time, I finished my education in two other programs on mastering management and leadership skills at Landmark and ExecuNet.Inc. I mentally reviewed my journey and how many conferences and workshops I had attended to broaden my horizons! I learn from many experts in the field. I felt gratitude to my bones for everyone who supported me in pursuing my dream and believed in me! Many times, in my journey, I felt overwhelmed by having to stretch my capabilities and personal limitations, but I never gave up. Many days were difficult, and I faced setbacks, as I have to do things repeatedly in order to build positive habits and processes. But I felt satisfied that I used the famous determination and fire within me, the determination and persistence that I am famous for, to stick with my goals, even though no one in my family believed that I would achieve them.

I reviewed my goals for the day, and as usual, I finished the five projects that I intended to complete for the day. I felt satisfied (the rule of five that I learned from my mentor Jack Canfield). Then I reviewed my long-term goals and what next steps to take. I used mind-mapping so that my determination met my clarity and passion so that the beauty prevailed. I knew in my bones that the road to be a bigger person did not stop there. As I reviewed my route, something else landed in my lap! To further update my skills and put all my energy, time, and money in pursuing it, I took "The Train a Trainer Program for Success Principles" by Jack Canfield Institute. At the same time, I was introduced to the Mary Morrissey Life Mastery Institute for Life Coaching. I was programming and laying out how to handle these large projects and plan in detail what steps I needed to do every day to succeed. As the law of attraction works, I put love out there, and love came back to me! The journey took six months for both projects to prevail. I stretched myself more and more so I would be comfortable outside of my comfort zone. Many times, my family wanted me to give up, and it was not an easy road. I spent all my money, time, sleepless nights, and energy to pursue my dream. I faced many setbacks but never gave up.

I live out of my comfort zone every day as everything is a new concept from what I've previously done. It took a great deal of courage, resilience, and determination to learn and comprehend these new concepts of being, living, and enjoying. It's a whole new level, and indeed, I put everything I had to update my skills so I could serve the community in the best possible way and give back to those who backed me even on the worst days. I used all my curiosity and compassion to learn to live and teach the Success Principles that I learned from Canfield's methodology and the physical, emotional, and spiritual parts of being and doing from Mary Morrissey.

After that, I completed the Columbia University Business School for Business/Executive Coaching and Executive Education of Leadership and Management. Together, these results were formidable and gave me a whole new level to live and enjoy my passion for being in service. The results of all that hard work and determination are indescribable, and the fulfillment and gratitude that I learned in the process are extraordinary.

One of the most common causes of failure is quitting when one is overtaken by temporary defeat.

— Napoleon Hill

EXAMPLE

"Good morning, Mom," Arthur greeted me.

"Good morning, my love. Did you have a good sleep?"

"Yes, Mom. What are you doing, Mom?"

"Studying, Arthur. I've got to finish this project, as there is a deadline."

"Mom, when will you finish studying? How do you get all this energy and focus? Moms your age do not do that anymore, please!"

"Yes, Arthur." I smiled and hugged my son. "When you love something, or someone, are you going the extra mile to do what it takes to get it done?"

"Yes, Mom, but you are too much. I wish I were like you."

I hugged him again and served his breakfast as we discussed the day's schedule.

"Mom, can you help me focus because I have a big homework assignment to finish?"

"Yes, my love, certainly!"

As we went through the homework, I repeated the same exercise twenty times to make sure he understood since he had difficulty comprehending it, and in the end, we completed the project. "Mom, how on earth! You don't give up but keep going through twenty times for the same concept! Wow, Mom, you have such patience and determination; I wish I were like you!"

Smiling, I hugged him. He means the world to me, and I would do anything and everything to help him succeed, be healthy, and happy.

ACTION STEPS

You're trying to figure out: "How have I been letting this person down? How have I been getting in the way?"

- Is it clear what needs to get done? How can I make the goals or expectations clearer?

- Is the level of quality that's required for this work precise? What examples or details can I provide to clarify the level of quality that's needed?

- Am I respectful of the amount of time I have to accomplish something? Can I be doing a better job of protecting my time?

- Do I feel I'm being set up to fail in any way? Are my expectations realistic? What am I asking that we should adjust, so it's more reasonable?

- Do I have the tools and resources to do my job well?

- Have I been given enough context about why this work is important, who the work is for, or any other crucial information to do my job well?

- What's irked me or rubbed me the wrong way about the management style? Does the tone come off the wrong way? Does management follow up too frequently with me, not giving me space to breathe?

Ask these questions to look outward.

You're trying to figure out: "What on the employee's end is limiting them? What choices or capabilities of their own are keeping them from the results you want to see?"

- How have I been feeling about my performance lately? Where do I see opportunities to improve, if any?

- What am I most enjoying about the work I'm doing? What part of the work is inspiring, motivating, and energizing, if any?

- What part of the work do I feel stuck in? What have I been trying the "crack the nut" on, but it feels like I'm banging my head?

- What part of the work is "meh"? What tasks have I felt bored or ambivalent?

- When's the last time I got to talk to or connect with a customer who benefited from the work I did? Would I like more opportunities to do that, and should I make that happen?

- Do I feel I'm playing to my strengths in my role? Where do I feel like there is a steep learning curve?

- Would I say I'm feeling optimistic, pessimistic, or somewhere in the middle about the company's future?

You'll notice that none of these questions ask, "What do you think you're doing wrong?" or "What do you think I'm doing wrong?" The point of these questions is not to end up in an accusatory place, either way. Your goal is to reach a place of better understanding. By approaching the conversation with an underperforming employee with questions to ask, rather than answers or directives to insert, you create space for you and your employee to do something different to change and improve. That change and that improvement is the goal, after all.

Determination and persistence distinguish extraordinary thinking, being, and living from ordinary thinking, being, and living.

— Desi Tahiraj

CHAPTER 14

Essentials of Leadership
- Character and Disputes

Essentially, leadership begins from within. It's the small voice that tells you where to go when you feel lost. If you believe in your inner voice, you believe in yourself.
— Azim Freaji

From the moment I open my eyes in the morning until I go to sleep, I make hundreds of decisions, and days, months, and years pass by, and my habits are created. In the business world and everyday life, we make business decisions and negotiations. There are small decisions like whether to have tea or coffee with breakfast, implement the new platform in our operating system, or the new branch office budget. Most of the time, we operate in that continual urge to get something, buy something, sell something, convince someone, buy the best car, home, vacation, or the latest gadget, and never take a moment to look at how small we treat our lives!

As self-centered creatures, we believe that our rational and judgmental decisions are the best way to go. Most of the time, we ignore that little voice inside telling us that something is not right, but we miss it, and the adverse happens, the setback or the project fails, or you have a dispute with your coworker or spouse, and on and on. The fight then escalates to the point that our ego gets the upper hand and they don't let us see clearly, so our fight-or-flight mode operates until one or the other wins or proves its point! It is sad and tragic that we as humans have lost touch with our inner beauty. We are spiritual beings. No matter how hard a façade someone puts up in the workplace, under that surface resides a beautiful and fragile soul that wants peace and happiness. Show me compassion, and empathy, and willingness to hear other points of view to save a relationship, project, or anything else that I undertake. I listen to that little voice inside me trying to tell me something and equalize my heart, inner voice, and head on every decision I make. Before I decide something, I ask whether this decision is right for everyone and whether it will benefit the department or business. Asking for feedback is the most effective way to collaborate and bring the spirit of a mission to everyone. By doing so, I motivate my team, show leadership and humility to be inclusive, and show my commitment to the cause. Sometimes our heart's decision is more robust than our conscious brain; other times, our conscious brain is more vital than our heart's decision. I have experienced both scenarios, and I learned that I need to integrate my three parts of being—my spiritual, logical, and emotional beings—when I make an educated decision. I have to make an informed decision on how it will affect everyone and whether the decision is one for the greater good. Remember that no one operates in a vacuum; we are part of our family, community, organization, and church. So, every decision I make needs to align with the community's values to which I belong.

I found that meditation is vital for aligning my inner and outer self to clarify a situation, as the brain goes from fight-or-flight mode to clear and rational, and I make the right decision as I look beyond my feet, when I don't rush to answer but instead sit on it to gain a deeper understanding, I learned that I move from responding instantly to an educated response. Give this approach a try, and I'm sure you will be glad you did so.

EXAMPLE

By listening to my heart and inner voice, not just my head, I can make a massive difference in how I live and thrive. I should approach life's challenges and opportunities with a welcoming and gracious mindset because I grow and build happiness for everyone through them.

It was morning. I was working on the five projects that I intended to finish and based on the schedule; I just finished the first one. I switched gears to start the second project and suddenly, I received an email that requested me to enroll in an online class about something that I had no clue what it was, but it would help me with the business. I didn't feel right and my gut told me not to enroll. I pondered it; in an hour, I received a second email for the same thing, and then a third. Then I thought that: "I am supposed to do it as there had to be a reason to request this so demandingly." So I went on and purchased the online course. I felt something was not right—a feeling in all my being that it was not what I wanted to do. However, because I thought that there had to be a reason behind the demand, perhaps it was a good thing. I opened the curriculum, and it didn't grab my attention, or curiosity, or even feel right! *Oh,* I said, *maybe this is because of my limiting beliefs that I think that way! I will do something else now and come back to this one project tomorrow.* I went on to do other tasks, and the next day, I went back to that program that I had purchased the day before. Did it attract me at all? Not at all. It was nonsense. Guess what? I didn't do that program that day, the week later, the month after, or the month after that. I never finished!

I realized that I should have listened to the gut feeling telling me not to purchase it. It was a defining moment as I realized that when something you don't like to do or something does not align with what your inner self means, something is trying to warn you. I learned a big lesson that by listening to the little voice that was warning me, I could have saved time, money, and energy! How many of us can relate to this story? It happens every day to all of us. The questions below are a perfect illustration that we all can apply in our everyday lives and succeed.

ACTION STEPS

Strategy and Mindset Priority List

Strategic Direction

Do I know where to start?
Do I know how to do this?
Do I know what to do first?
What is first? Do I know what to do?
What does my inner voice tell me to do? Call it gut or intuition. My GPS.
Create a space for my inner voice to come through.
Use the quiet time to help guide me toward my authentic expression.
Pay attention to my emotions and body sensations.

Bridge Strategy & Mindset

I don't always speak my mind!
I always speak my mind – I overthink.
I'm not the most patient person!
I have a hard time asking for help!
I have a hard time delegating a task!

Irritability Triggers

Irritability is a struggle with pride and the expectations of others.
What irritates me?
What do I need to do to fix it?
Who could I ask for help?
How I stop yourself from asking?

Discomfort

Do I procrastinate on the task?
Am I afraid or nervous?
Do I feel it aligns with my priorities?
Weakness / Solution / Action Steps

Fact: People-challenges contribute to over 70% of change failure factors.

Our mind is like a muscle; the more you exercise it, the more it can expand.

Be still. The quieter you become, the more you can hear.

— Ram Bass

CHAPTER 15

Align with Your Tribe –
Fight the Ego

You cannot negotiate with people who say what's mine is mine, and what's yours is negotiable!
— John F. Kennedy

While we hear about tragedies and crises worldwide, we are usually so close-minded and self-centered that we barely see other people's needs. The paradox is that I need that other person to be the best I can be. As humans, have we been built to be together from the beginning of time, and from that, we created families, communities, organizations, corporations, states, and countries? We are all parts of a whole and being aware of this reality is vital so that all our lives have meaning. I must come to my senses, see the big picture, and become self-aware that my egotism is just a weakness that consciously or unconsciously moves me out of alignment with my family, community, and organization. It's like a domino effect: if I do not notice what is around me and consciously choose to get out of that fight-or-flight mode, I will find myself as a free electron that is destined to demolish itself. Unfortunately, this issue is prominent everywhere. I must remind the person infected with such a high dose of misery and fear (egotism) and help them gain perspective and move from being out of alignment and fulfillment without letting this poison drag the person down. As humans, it comes down to our self-awareness and choice to feed or not feed it. However, this is easier said than done because this flaw based on fear and the need to survive. It's not easy to cure; there needs to be a new way to approach it directly and indirectly. After all, this is the beauty of being human as we discover more and more about ourselves.

EXAMPLE

Tuesday morning and Ted was struggling to prepare for the 11 a.m. meeting. He felt pressure, fear, and regret that he didn't design the report a week ago, and he didn't know where to start. He thought that he shouldn't have gone out to drink several nights in a row or spend his time shopping for things he didn't need. But now, what could he do? He remembered that he saw Jack the other day working on the same project and was teasing him about being an office freak! He ran to Jack's cubicle and asked, "Hey Jack, what's going on with the report you were preparing for the change in algorithm for the new software? Did you find the combination code that could work?" "Oh, yes, I did!" Jack replied. "May I see it so that we can be on the same page in the meeting?" Jack opened his folder and let Ted peek at the computer screen. Ted's eyes were shining as he tried to screenshot the info with his gaze. He tried not to show his emotions and stammered, "That is great.... I didn't have time." Jack found Ted's behavior awkward and said, "That is fine. Okay, I've got to get back to work. See you later." "Yes, sure, thanks!" Ted said, and left. Sure enough, Ted ran to his office and filled out the info he had just seen on Jack's computer screen. He felt relieved and thought that he could handle the meeting with the department head and all six team members. Ted rushed to make the first presentation. He presented Jack's finding, which stunned Jack, who couldn't believe that Ted would do that! Jack tried to calm himself and not focus on what a jerk Ted was. The boss congratulated Ted for doing a great job, and Ted never mentioned that Jack had helped him. The meeting ended with the manager asking for a few changes and outlining what needed to be done by the team members before the next meeting. As you might imagine, Jack and Ted avoided each other for the rest of the week!

ACTION STEPS

When situations like what I've just described happen in a professional setting, step back, breathe, and take a moment before you speak.

- Try to understand the other person's real motives.

- Have the willpower to step out of your reptilian brain.

- Evaluate and understand the nuances of the other person's motives.

- Ask the other person for information and be honest and explain why you are bothered by what he or she has done.

- If you are at fault, authentically apologize, and acknowledge that your ego and fear often block you. Honestly express your willingness to solve the issue and produce an outcome that will be positive for everyone.

- Be compassionate with others and treat them the way you want to be treated.

At other times our ego shows up in many forms and shapes, sometimes camouflaged and sometimes not, but recognize that it can often alienate family members, coworkers, associates, and others. The opposite of this situation is when we align with our true nature and are aware of our alignment with our inner and outer self, with our family, community, coworkers, and organization. See things in perspective and recognize that egotism is destructive and needs to be demolished for the greater good. Authentically, we align ourselves with empathy, apologize to the person we hurt, and not repeat it in the future. That is what it means to be a powerful human.

Be aware that we pay the price for not keeping agreements.

• Loss of trust; loss of respect
• Loss of relationships
• Loss of business, jobs, income, money
• Tiredness, fatigue, loss of energy
• Confusion, lack of mental clarity, lack of inner peace
• Loss of integrity; loss of self-esteem
• Loss of power

Here are some tips for making fewer agreements and for keeping the ones you make.

1. Make only agreements that you intend to keep. Take a few seconds before agreeing to see if it is what you want to do. Check in with yourself. How does your body feel about it? Do not compromise on anything just because you are looking for someone's approval. If you do, you'll find yourself breaking these commitments.

2. Write down all the agreements you make. Use a calendar, daily planning book, notebook, or computer to record all of your arrangements. One of the big reasons we don't keep our contracts is that we forget many of the agreements we have made because of the daily pressure surrounding our activities.
Write them down, and then review your list every day. When we don't write something down or make an effort to store these things in our long-term memory, the memory will be lost in as little as 37 seconds.

3. Communicate any broken agreements at the first appropriate time. As soon as you know you will have a broken agreement—your car won't start, you're stuck in traffic, your child is sick—notify the other person as soon as possible. It demonstrates respect for others' time and their needs.

4. Clarify that you have agreements with other people, so you both have the same understanding.

5. Learn to say no more often. Give yourself time to think it over before making any new agreements. I write the word NO in yellow highlighter on all my calendar pages as a way to remind myself to consider what else I'll have to give up if I say yes to something new. It makes me pause and think before I add another commitment to my life.

Behaviors to be aware of your triggers:
Showing disrespect for others
Increase in risk-taking/accidents
Senseless arguments with others
Increased use of tobacco, alcohol, coffee, drugs
Excessively active or underactive
Aggressive/passive aggression
Being unreasonably demanding
Having angry outbursts
Difficulty starting or finishing
Refusal to take time off
Withdrawing socially
Difficulty communicating
A decline in performance
Difficulty in concentrating

Self-leadership and personal development are a must if you wish to have a healthy, happy, and successful life. We all develop from the day we were born to the day we die. Take a leap and do things that serve you and everyone else, even if it is uncomfortable at the beginning, and I guarantee you will prevail.

PART III

OPEN TO NEW POSSIBILITIES

Life is a matter of choices, and every choice you make makes you.
— John C. Maxwell

CHAPTER 16

How to Make Educated Choices & Manage Your Outcomes

Make Good Choices Today So You Don't Have Regrets Tomorrow!

Choices! We don't realize it, but every second of the day, we make choices. Being aware of our choices is fundamental and critical to how we live and how we affect others. We make choices about what we think and feel, how we act, what new skills to learn, how to find positive solutions, the music we listen to, the friends we make, the homes we buy, the sports we like, what we eat, and just about every other aspect of our lives. The list of choices we make goes on and on. The point is that most of the time, we make choices without thinking or without being aware of the impact of our choices. We do the best we can from the level of our consciousness. However, making educated choices is essential if we want to have positive results more often than not. Before I was choosing whatever came up in life and my surrounding circumstances, and that made me feel powerless and like a victim. Even I noticed that the choice I made was a mistake that would cause a significant loss. I surrendered, and indeed, I paid the price! The paradox is that I was blaming circumstances. That was until I learned the success principles from my mentor Mr. Jack Canfield! An enormously powerful yet simple formula that I follow is: Event plus your Response equals the Outcome. I think of the outcome as what I want to achieve and respond accordingly and raise my self-awareness!

ACTION STEPS

I have seen repeatedly that most people do not think about the impact of their response when they reply to someone. They may consider it for a moment, but people must try to see the result of their response or decision on family, team members, an organization, and themselves in the long run.

- Do you feel that you sometimes give a quick answer without considering your response and then regret something you've said or did?

- Or should you have said something but instead said nothing?

- Are you mad about one coworker and complain to another colleague instead of speaking to the first person? Or do you go home and complain to your spouse about your coworker?

- Are you mad about your spouse and go to work the next day and complain to your friend?

- Do you choose to sleep a few extra minutes and show up late for an appointment but complain about getting stuck in traffic?

- Have you chosen to ignore or not respond to the feedback that your supervisor or coworkers gave you, and then you were fired?!

We experience annoyance or discontent in our family relationships, but we often fail to address them! We often are unwilling to confront people or be honest with ourselves as it is uncomfortable or inconvenient. We forget that if we engage with empathy and mutual understanding, our results will be more positive than we think as perhaps the other side is waiting for that something!

EXAMPLE I

I met Elea at an event, and I noticed her personality and warm nature. At the lunch break, she invited me to her table, and I accepted. As we were eating and having a pleasant conversation, I noticed a change in her voice and her eye expression that signaled melancholy and discontent! I asked whether something was bothering her, and she started to cry. "Did I say something wrong?" "No," she said. "I am just so fed up with my husband, and I can't take it any longer. It's been this way for many years. We are millions of miles apart, but we're still living under the same roof. I shouldn't have married him. It was a mistake, a bad decision, and I'm living with the outcome every day. What do you think I should do?" she asked in a sinking voice. "Well, since you asked, did you have this conversation with your husband and discuss what your concerns or requests are?" "No. I am avoiding it. It is not easy!" she whispered. "Well, this is a mature conversation and is not comfortable. However, it will better for both of you if you have a heart-to-heart conversation. You don't know what the response will be. Perhaps your husband notices all this as well, and you can come up with a solution!"

EXAMPLE II

Carl showed up in my office as soon as I opened the door that morning. "May I speak with you?" "Certainly, come in. What's up?" I asked. "Well, I am annoyed and fed up with Ken. He drives me nuts every day, and you need to move him to another office so I can work!" "Oh, why?" "Well, his office and mine are separated by a partial wall, and he speaks loudly on the phone or brings in his team members for meetings in his office, and the noise disturbs me so much." "Did you speak with Ken?" "Yes, I did, but he ignored me, and his tone was so angry!" "How was your tone of voice" "What relationship do you want to have with Ken?" I asked. "In the beginning, everything was fine, but now he has five people on his team, and they make a lot of noise, and I went there angry, and shouted at them! "What relationship do you wish to have with Ken, and what outcome do you wish to have from your conversation? Did you discovered why he ignored you?" "Yes, he was mad that I went directly to his lab members and complained directly to them!"

"There are many ways to fix this situation. Do you think you would speak to Ken first before approaching his lab members, so things are under control? Do you want me to speak with Ken? Remember, there are also conference rooms where meetings can be held."

"No, I changed my mind; I will speak with him again!"

"Okay. Just keep in mind what we discussed."

"Okay, I will go to meet him right now; I will let you know. Thank you."

A few hours later, Carl showed up in my office again. "Hi, Carl. What's new now?"

"Oh, when I went back to my office, I thought that I was a bit of a jerk and probably was rude to Ken. I met with Ken, apologizing to him for being rude, and we found a solution. He will use the conference room when he meets with his team. I just came here to thank you for helping me to see and realize and open ways for communication and offering a solution. I almost burned a relationship with my colleague!"

"You're welcome, Carl."

When he left, I felt happy that everyone was okay and running smoothly in the office. We must give all our heart, knowledge, work, and devotion to helping the organization prosper and make sure the community thrives, the family grows, and that we have contributed all we can to look for prosperity and high performance.

To make educated choices, you might ask yourself the following questions:

- How will this choice affect me in the short term?
- What would the immediate effects of my choice be?
- What ramifications could this have for me today, tomorrow, next week, next month, or even a year from now?
- How will it help me now?
- **How would it hurt me now?**
- Are there any possibilities that I haven't explored yet?
- Who else can I ask that may have the experience to help me with this choice?
- Figuring out how a choice will affect you now can help you to decide whether the choice is even a viable option.
- **How will this choice affect me in the long term?**
- How will this choice affect me down the road?
- Will you experience the effects of today's decision a year from now, five years from now, or ten years from now?
- **Will this choice result in something professional or worthwhile?**
- Are there any immediate or long-term benefits that could lead me or my business to a place of enhanced professionalism as a result of making this choice?
- Will the results be worthwhile?
- Often, we face choices that seem like they are good ideas but then realize down the road that those choices did not lend themselves to creating a professional image, additional revenue, or achievement of any specific goals.

- Is this choice consistent with my goals?
- Consistency is a crucial component of success. If you don't currently have your goals written down, I would highly recommend doing so before making significant choices for yourself or your business. Use the mind-mapping technique and the rule of five. When we make educated choices for the benefit of our health, relationships, careers, community, family, and organization, we live a life of prosperity and fulfillment for the greater good for all, and this is a blessing.

Use Six Psychological Truths for an Educated Decision

1. Framing – Loss-Gain Mindset
2. Vividness – Recency Effect
3. Stereotyping – Mental Shortcuts / Generalizations
4. Anchoring – The Power of the First / Actions
5. Confirmation – Selective Attention
6. Escalations – Defend and Justify

These are the six psychological truths that we must be aware of when it comes to effective decision-making. DISCUSSING how critical self-awareness is a starting place for actively growing your ability to lead effectively and influence others in a meaningful way.

Do 5 Things Every Day to Gain Clarity

Find what matters to you.

Prioritize quiet time

We schedule all of the "important" things in our life. We are always an app away on our computer, phone, or tablet to see what's happening this week, and we follow it. Utilize the structures you already have in your life, and schedule in QUIET TIME. Schedule it in and hold it like all your other events that you never miss.

Try new things, big or small.

In my experience, clarity comes from saying "no" more and "yes" less, but that does not mean shutting new things out of your life. It means trying new things, big things, small things, any things like no cream in your coffee for a week.

Write down the five things you are going to do today.

Clarity today comes pretty easy if you have a list. Take a plan to the next level by narrowing it to five things. Please put them in order of importance, and DO NOT start #2 until #1 is complete!

Clean your space.

I mean, it is self-explanatory; a clean desk, bedside table, kitchen, closet, or pantry make you feel like a whole new person. Clutter weighs on us more than we think. If you have a lot to clean up around you, just start with a small space where you spend most of your time.

Find what matters to you.

Who you are, what is important to you sometimes slips by, and you stop and think to yourself "wait, what do I care about?" Real life has a way of keeping us distracted, and then boom, you're working a job you hate, with a partner you don't love, or a lifestyle that no longer serves you. My belief and my work are designed around the concept that what truly drives us are our values. Our values are identifiable, measurable, and experienced in our daily lives, therefore finding clarity of what our values are, what they mean, and how they manifest in our behavior is the most powerful way of finding clarity in our lives.

CHAPTER 17

How to Find the Beauty in Everyone

I think human beings make life beautiful. There's a lot of beauty in everything. I think what makes life beautiful is the ability to acknowledge that.
— Andrew McMahon

The beauty of human nature fascinates me every time I think of it! Our creation is magic, and when one thinks of that it is a happy place to live, as every moment is a treasure. Considering that we all have a spirit, and that we live our human experiences most brilliantly is a miracle. Imagine we collect all our thoughts, our dreams, our experiences in one collective place, and we all watch that movie of all of us at the same time! How fascinating would that be! Since I was a child, I was a good listener and observer. Indeed, everyone was interpreting life differently for the same event they all witnessed, and that is fascinating! Imagine for a moment if every one of us thinks the same thing, speaks the same thing, eats the same thing, dreams the same thing, and does the same thing. How boring life would be!

By thinking and living this beautiful life, we live a life full of empathy and wisdom. When we allow the adverse to happen, we tend to disconnect from ourselves and others. I notice and am aware of my thoughts, stay in touch with my gut feelings, and follow the good. I will see that any problem disappears and repeatedly see that empathy and love are within me to the end. As I know, I cannot think a thought without my body reacting. Think about that. We are wired to be with each other, so I treat the other person just like I want to be treated; I love to discover the beauty that lies in every one of us and bring that up and feed it so that we can live a life of loving. If I take time and see and hear the other person, I will find that greatness resides inside all of us. I am patient and understanding with any misunderstanding, so I do not end up in a "power talk" that one or the other is right or wrong, as we just come from different paradigms. When I argue with my coworker, boss, spouse, or children, I pause for a breath and ask myself *who am I? What is the best outcome for everyone? Is this something that needs to be addressed?*

Set your boundaries with empathy and understanding for both sides, and remember we are humans living together in this beautiful heaven we call Earth!

EXAMPLE

Arthur had just come back from school, and as he greeted me and went to clean up, I was preparing his lunch! "Arthur, lunch is ready," I called.

"Bring it to my room," he answered.

"No, my love, come in the kitchen so we can share and talk." He wasn't happy, and with an unpleasant face, he sat down at the table and started eating.

"Mom, I don't like that you are writing a book. English is your second language, and there are a lot of people out there better than you."

"Yes!" I answered, as I felt the worry and disbelief in his voice. "I know there are many people out there, but no one like your mom! Every one of us has our fingerprints, and I just want to put my thoughts on paper and hopefully help someone else prevent the cost of burnout in any way possible."

"Mom, please get an office job. For that, you are good, as you are a workaholic. Don't spend your time with this. I just can't see you any longer without a job."

I felt his pain, and I understood what he was talking about. I felt his anger, worry, and the rudeness in his voice, but I did not take it wrong as that was his point of view and said with good intent.

"I got you, and I see that you don't see me as a good writer, and you just want to play it safe for our security. I understand. Just believe me for once."

"No, Mom, I don't trust you any longer as you don't keep your promise. You told me that you would start to work last month and the month before that."

I felt his hurt and insecurity and worry. "Everything will be okay, Art. I promise."

"OK, Mom," he said, and left for his room. It was a solemn moment for me, but I knew that he just meant well from his perspective and did not intend to hurt me. It's what it means to be wise, empathetic, and understanding and take in the beauty of the other person and be agile at the same time. I washed the dishes and went back to write the book, as I knew that I was doing it not for me; it helped hundreds and thousands of other people prevent burnout and live with love and care to the deepest level of abundance and happiness. What it is to be a powerful human, to come out of your little self, serve and help as many people as possible, be entirely in service of others, and surrender yourself to the eternity and goodness in the world. That is the beauty of human nature that we need to look for and nurture in every single person as it's God's blessings. Inner beauty is the permanent truth. Inner beauty defines who I am as a person and empowers outer beauty. Inner beauty is a divine essence that cannot be manufactured; it only is created from within. That is, how do we embrace and enhance our inner beauty?

By looking at the world without judging or interpreting. By surrounding ourselves with people who will bring us up, encourage us to move forward, and maintain our outer beauty in the metaphoric and business worlds. We all experience setbacks and downtime along the road, but we feel that the fire and curiosity inside us keep our dream alive! Our creativity, our quest to fulfill our deepest desires, entitle us to experience and be in use for a greater good for all! Let's explore what you could do to ignite your fire and your curiosity that will develop habits, practices, and procedures that thrive. For example:

- Write down goals and outcomes that you, as an executive, manager, or employee, want to achieve. What innovation will you ignite and implement for a Greater Good?
- Each objective has three to five key results. Each essential product should be a way to define success and measure progress toward success.
- Write down what you are missing in your thinking or procedures that need to be upgraded and make the action plan with the time frame.
- Practice everyday meditation to keep you grounded with tasks at hand for the next sixty-six days.
- Ask the person that you think could help you with this quest tomorrow. Use coaching.
- Every Friday, write the steps you took that week, the results you got, and upgrade or change the steps along away to help you improve.

- What is your unique time management system that makes you feel sure that you have time for success?
- What tasks do you delegate and how do you do that?
- Do you focus on what is essential and not worry about the rest?
- Create a template and allow others to display their genius.
- Use mind mapping and the Rule of Five to stay focused and productive.
- Organize a run, a marathon, a picnic or any activity that brings your team together.
- How open are you to other people's ideas, different cultures and different races?
- Who is your hero and why, as you will discover your strengths?
- What thinking, behaviors and other patterns do I need to change to produce the results I want? How will I deliver the wow factor for the customer?
- Am I curiosity about what drives the other person's behavior? Will curiosity and empathy approach open the light for me and the other person to find a solution and move forward?

The love of beauty in its multiple forms is the noblest gift of the human cerebrum!
— **Alexis Carrel**

CHAPTER 18

The Gift of Saying "NO" is Not Against Others – It's for You!

**The art of leadership is saying no, not saying yes.
It is very easy to say yes.
— Tony Blair**

I learned to say "no" in a challenging way, and the funny part is that I found out that it did not hurt anyone, as everyone is replaceable. You see, every one of us is born into different circumstances and environments, and in my case, saying "no" meant that I didn't care about the other person or teammate! As a heart-centered person, I put my heart in everything I do, including when I held my son in my lap every night for about four years as he could not breathe when lying down. Food, doctors, cleaning, bills, buying and selling the house, my ex-husband's health, my parents' and sisters' needs, and the work around everyone's issues and requests even if it was not my job. If someone was lacking, I jumped in to finish! It's the calling that every employee or leader needs to be happy and well cared for, so we all prosper. That was fundamentally wrong. I remember that my outstanding chairman used to tell me, "Please, Desi, learn to say *no*...we need you!" How right he was, as it has nothing to do with the other person; it is just for you. I had to understand that when we tend to do too much for everyone's sake to be safe and well, in business or with family, we get burnt out ourselves. It is not selfish to say *no* if it means to take care of ourselves, as what is right for anyone if you get burned out? The thing we need to distinguish is when and how to say *no*. That is critical, and it comes with self-awareness, wisdom, developing leadership skills and learning from others that went before you in that path that would ultimately save us from making the same mistakes. At that time, I didn't know the fundamental knowledge, the difference between Attachment vs. Commitment! Indeed, one day I became burned out, to the extent that I couldn't handle it anymore! I left everything and went deep down to study and understand what causes high achievers to burn out, and that saying *yes* to everything is a massive part of it!

You see, as human creatures, our internal need is to be likable and acceptable at home to our parents, siblings, school, job, community, and on and on! We adjust ourselves to fit into society and incorporate it into our lives. Based on our personal DNA and paradigm, we develop a certain level of awareness and thinking that is unique for each of us, and it is incredible how much influence our choices and decisions have. Our need to fit into society, family, careers, and friendships leads us many times to say yes even when we often want to say *no*, which is inauthentic and does not help anyone on any level. Awareness, meditation, mindfulness, and studying are critical and helped me become aware of my limitations and wanting to be needed. Authentically and with empathy, I would have a conversation with the person who is asking me to say *yes* and check the tone that I am using when I say *no*, and I keep in mind that when I say *no* it is not against them, it is for me! I keep in mind that there are pushers that push me continuously about something that is not my job or on something for which I do not have time, or for any other reasons, and with empathy, I just say, "I won't be able to do that right now."

ACTION STEPS

You will save yourself with integrity and dignity by doing so, and you will be helping yourself and everyone in your community. We are creatures of habit, so it is easier said than done. Do yourself a favor and get out of that comfort zone and check out how often you say *yes* when the time and circumstances suggest you should say *no*; this is a skill worth mastering if you wish to lead a less stressful life.

- *I am unable to take this on as I am in the middle of several other projects.*

If you are already full up and busy with several projects, you simply do not have the time for anything more.

- *Give me some time to think about it, and I'll get back to you.*

Sometimes saying no straightaway becomes difficult and requesting time can solve your problem of saying no, at least for the moment.

- *I am not taking additional responsibilities for the moment.*

You are making it clear that your projects and other commitments, both business and personal, are keeping you busy.

- *I'd love to do this, but unfortunately, I cannot commit myself.*

It's an excellent way of saying no to someone you do not want to get involved with. "This does not meet my requirements, but I'll keep you in mind." If someone is pressuring you to accept a deal that does not meet your needs, you should not hesitate to say so without prolonging the matter any further.

- *You can do it yourself.*

Too often, we come across people who come running for help when they can do the job themselves.

- *Unexpected things have cropped up that need my immediate attention.*

Due to unavoidable circumstances, you cannot take on the project, and no is the answer. So, what do we do? The secret is in the art of saying the forbidden word—no.

- *Polite but firm.*

Being polite is essential while refusing. Politely. However, remember to be firm.

- *Don't give too many explanations. Saying no when you feel like it is your right, so don't offer too many reasons for the refusal.*

Try these techniques to liberate you and everyone around you and help the business grow.

"Just saying yes because you can't bear the short-term pain of saying no is not going to help you do the work."
— Seth Godin

The truth is self-care plays a significant role in feeling good and being resilient during difficult times. I'd like to share simple and effective ways to get your brain in the "habit" of self-care. But don't take my word for it - never do with anyone. Try these simple nurturing actions for yourself right now and see what you notice.

1. Start your morning by thinking of five things you're grateful for

2. Practice mindful eating or drinking for a few minutes during a meal or a coffee/tea break.

3. Try a mindful check-in once or twice during the day.

4. Take at least a 20-minute walk each day to care for your body.

5. Put your hands on your heart for a moment to wish yourself well. Try saying the words: "May I be healthy and happy."

6. If things get tough, acknowledge that it's a difficult moment, and in life, everyone has them, and consciously keep your inner critic at bay.

7. At night, look back on the day, forgive all the people you're holding grudges against (yourself included), release the burden, and settle in for a good night's sleep.

CHAPTER 19

The Only Person You Can Change is You

Everyone thinks of changing the world, but no one thinks of changing himself.
— Leo Tolstoy

When I was young, I was thinking of changing the world. I grew up a little, and I said I would change my city. I grew up a little more, and then I said I would change my family. Then I grew up more, and I realized that the only person I could change is me. I was judging myself for "not being good enough," hahaha! Does this sound familiar to you? I judged my coworker for being a winner, and I tried to "help" by being more positive and proactive, hahaha! Did that happen with you too? I was judging complainers and trying to teach them not to! Hahaha! Did you do that also?

I judged my ex-husband for his weakness, and I tried to "fix" him, hahaha! Did that happen with you too?

I was judging my sister and tried to fix her thinking, hahaha! Did that happen to you too?

I was judging my son for being irresponsible and procrastinating, hahaha! Did you do that too?

Guess what? I ended up realizing that the only person who needs to change is me.

So, I started a three-year journey to make changes from living inside the box to living outside the box, from having a fixed mindset to a growth mindset! Indeed, that requires a lot of will, discipline, and determination, and the results are unmatched! I could not describe the satisfaction, fulfillment, and enlightenment as I now live my life more powerfully! It is fascinating how everything changes when we change our thinking and the pictures we carry in our minds about people and reality; it's just a paradigm we live in. When we change our perception and change from a fixed mindset to a growth mindset, it brings groundbreaking awareness and mindfulness, and our life reflects that.

If we look in the mirror, the energy we put out there bounces back to us, and vice versa. However, most of the time, we get caught in our everyday routine and are mindless in the way we think, speak, and react; and we blame and complain about others when we hardly see ourselves in the mirror, and reflect and talk to ourselves honestly! Believing that I can thrive and be unbreakable only by upgrading my mindset, I set myself up for success.

ACTION STEPS

How can you change someone who doesn't see an issue in their actions?

- We affect others by way of our being and dealing with others, not asking them what to do or think!
- Engaging in conversation and offering suggestions with empathy, looking at the other person in the eye, and discussing with unspoken language and body movement are more important than what you say.

- Infuse your life with action, and don't wait for things to fall out of the sky!
- Make your future, infuse your hopes, and do what you love, what your inner voice tells you; just stop and listen!
- If I don't like something, I change it. If I can't change it, I change how I think about it, and I accept it and move on. The only way that I can change is to learn, apply, and start over from where I am with what I have, an open heart and open mind.

It's amazing how the law of attraction works; what you put out bounces back to you and is so powerful yet is just not comprehended by most of us!

- What if you write down a list tonight acknowledging all the people and events you resent or don't see the way to deal with and look into each of them and take a look at what you like or dislike?

- Write down the feelings you are experiencing. By writing everything down, the brain (our conscious and unconscious mind) reacts to the reflection you will see. You will realize that most of what you think is not right or is just the fear that triggers you. It's a fantastic exercise that anyone can use and be surprised, as I was.

I was the one who did not believe in such a thing! I was a lawyer, and it was everything for me to search for facts and clues. Let me tell you: I "was blown away" when I learned this concept!

- If you have been in a relationship for any length of time and you want to change the other person, well, get clear on one thing; you can't change other people.

- What I see is what I get, or should I say, what you have been witnessing for the time you have been in the relationship is what you will always get. People don't change! The only time people are willing to change is when they hit rock bottom.

- The person first has to believe that something wrong has to be changed, and they must be willing to put forth the effort to work at changing it. The only things you can change are your circumstances and yourself.

- Accept things as they are and stop trying to change someone because it merely isn't going to happen. The only person you can change is you!

- Self-awareness is fundamental to be aware of the limitations that prevent us from bringing abundance into our lives and business.

- Decide if what you have is what you want and if it is excellent. If not, make the changes necessary to begin to live your life the way you truly want.

- Ask yourself the hard question of WHY you feel that way without judging yourself. We tend to ignore the inner voice telling us that something is wrong, but we don't pay attention. Ask for help if you need it.

- Ask for feedback from your coworkers, boss, spouse, or siblings as their input or behaviors reflect our behavior. They are just trying to help you with a different point of view.

- Know your limits; we tend to take on our shoulders more than we could handle as we think that no one could do a better job than us. Perfection does not exist. Find the balance and delegate.

- Address in a timely manner any mess or problem that is lingering and we live unattended. If we do not clean up the clutter, then they become big problems.

- Be aware of any limiting beliefs or habits that are standing in the way and causing your burnout. We all have blind spots that we set ourselves up for a great burnout if we don't attend and change to empowering ones.

- Take a break to rejuvenate yourself and use this time to recover, step back and see your reflection; meditate for greater clarity. Give back to your family and community as giving is healing.

- Make educated choices using mindfulness and emotional intelligence to find the balance between the inner and outer selves.

- Recognize that you cannot change anyone. The only thing you could change is your thoughts, your vision that you keep in your mind, and your behaviors and actions to make an educated choice.

- Create a mastermind group, and everyone wins by having a different point of view and various options for solutions and accountability.

- Please reach out if you have any questions, as I would greatly appreciate any feedback you might have.

Solving issues at the workplace

In every organization, teamwork can be challenging as one understands the issue differently from another person, and the reverse happens. Here are the top tips that will help anyone have authentic relationships and build trust and profitability.

- When the adverse happens, step back, breathe, and pound before you speak.

- Be authentically curious to understand your real motives and the other party.

- Have the willpower to step out of your reptile brain.

- Evaluate and be real, so both parties see and work in differences.

- Understand the nuances of your point of view and another side as no one is right or wrong as it's only our perception and understanding of a certain way of reality.

- Give and request any information or feelings that bother you or the other person/team.

- Express full willingness to solve the issue that satisfies the outcome with facts and a positive effect.

- Be companionate with the others; the way you want to be treated.

- Always, as humans, we are wired to be with humans, so find that peace and come from that place, and you will see the issue is not an issue any longer.

- Authentically apologize and fight the ego that blocks you from doing so.

- Look at the issue or a problem without judging others or yourself; the solution will surface organically.

As my mentor Jack Canfield quoted: "You keep doing what you are doing, and you'll get the same results that you are getting." I would do anything to make you whole again, but I can't change your past, and only you can change NOW.

Let me know when you do and give me your feedback. 😊

CHAPTER 20

How to Leverage the Curiosity & Drive to Success

The Science of Curiosity leverages new knowledge, recognizes gaps, opens minds to people's ideas... Explore... New comes with stress... Accept it to Thrive.
— Dr. Stefan Oschmann, Merck

Did you ask yourself *who am I, and what purpose do I have?* I often ask myself that question, and I think that anyone or any company could benefit by doing that; it would address the question of "why" we exist as individuals or companies. Curiosity opens up a new perspective, ignites our purpose, and opens up a wide range of possibilities to any dream, issue, or project. And when it is channeled mindfully, by sharing and communicating, the results of anyone's personal development or any company milestone will be far easier to accomplish, as one says, "What mind can conceive and believe, man can achieve! When we are curious to learn more about any business matter or other people's problems or behaviors, we ask why they acted in the way they did, why this problem recurs, and why we process in the way we do. By posing the questions, we open ourselves to a wide range of possibilities and explore a better version of ourselves as a person or a business. Curiosity is timeless; it always was and always will be. It transcends race, religion, politics, finance, culture, bias, and prejudice. One way to know if curiosity is part of the fabric of your life is to look at how you live your life:

- What is working and what is not working—especially in these turbulent and challenging times?
- Is your life (personal, corporate) so mechanical that there is no room for curiosity or inquisitiveness?
- When was the last time you reinvented yourself, your business, your relationship?
- How do you feel about the notion of reinventing? Are you exhilarated, fearful?
- Curiosity is a personal conversation one has with one's self.

Many people today are having this conversation not only at mid-life but at quarter-life—from a lack of engagement, dissatisfaction, searching for a deeper meaning of life, or reevaluating their place in the grand scheme of things—fostering their curiosity.

ACTION STEPS

In organizations and relationships, each of these entities needs to engage in the exploration of change in order to thrive and prosper.

Curiosity supports the organization by looking with fresh eyes at opportunity, competitiveness, efficiency, and sustainability.

Curiosity supports relationships by looking with fresh eyes at their aliveness, spontaneity, maturation, connection, joy, happiness, and bliss.

- By posing a question to myself on a personal level or business level for any issue or solution to any project, I hear my inner voice, my "why?" that must study to get the knowledge that I need and ask around if I don't know.

- By being open to other people's ideas, I extend my awareness. I find the gap between where I was and where I want to be in my personal development and professionally. It took a lot of hard work and sleepless nights as new ideas come with stress, but I maintained practical meditation and breathing, invested in my passion, time, money, energy, and everything in between.

- Along the way, we all experience setbacks and downtime, but never give up that feeling of fire and curiosity inside us that keeps our dream alive! Our creativity, quest to fulfill our deepest desires that each of us is entitled to experience and use for a greater good!

Let's explore what we could do to ignite our fire and our curiosity that will develop habits, practices, and procedures that thrive.

- Write down goals and outcomes that you, as an executive, manager, or employee, want to achieve.

- Each objective has three to five key results. Each essential product should be a way to define success and measure progress toward success.

- Write down what you are missing in your thinking or the procedures you need to upgrade and make the action plan within a time frame.

- Practice everyday meditation to keep you keep grounded with tasks at hand for the next sixty-six days.

- Ask the person that you think could help you on this quest tomorrow and use their coaching.

- Every Friday, write the steps that you took that week, the results you got, and upgrade or modified steps along away to help you do better.

- What is your unique time management system that you are sure you have time for in order to achieve success?

- What and how do you delegate tasks?

- Do you focus on what is essential and not worry about the rest?

- Create a template and allow others to display their genius.

- Use mind-mapping and the Rule of Five to stay focused and productive.

- Organize a run/marathon/picnic or any activity that brings your team together.

- How open are you to other people's ideas, different cultures, and other races?

- Who is your hero and why, as you discover your strengths?

- What is your thinking and behavior, and your set of patterns and tendencies, to produce the results you want?

- Have curiosity about what drives the other person's behavior if interest and an empathetic approach turn on the light for you and the other person to find a solution to any issue or project. As humans, we are the most extraordinary creation that God brought into this world, and it is our job to look from the inside out and use the precious gift that was given to us for a better world with love and light! Go out there and emit the light! You're now facing one of the most challenging tasks as a leader.

- How do you manage underperformance at work? And more specifically, how do you sit down and talk about this underperformance?

- It's tempting to look outward first and to blame the person or extenuating circumstances: "They don't pay attention to detail."

- While those may very well be the case, you should also turn inward. As leaders, when an employee is underperforming, we must self-reflect. What are *you* doing that is stopping this person from doing their best work?

- The hard part about managing an underperforming employee is choosing to look *both* inward and outward for underperformance. What are you doing to hold an underperforming employee back? And what is the underperforming employee doing to hold herself back?

- Often, we think we know the answer to those questions. We have hunches about what's causing the underperformance: "It's their perfectionist tendency getting in the way" or "It's my lack of the project clarity."

- Coaching a struggling employee to success begins with asking the right questions, not merely arriving with the supposed answers.

- Feeling that others know them and understand their desires and goals helps maintain team cohesion and employee retention.

- Provide one idea to improve the product or service provided by your company. The best source of innovation is often from people who already work for you with ideas for improvement, no matter how big or how small.

- If you owned the company, what's one thing you would do differently? Ask this question to your employees once a month to encourage leadership from everyone in the company. You will make room to grow or change their management strategy. This way, you build performance without burning out as you build a strong foundation that resists this ever-changing world.

CHAPTER 21

Integrity & Productivity Within

With integrity, you have nothing to fear, since you have nothing to hide. With integrity, you will do the right thing, so you will have no guilt.
— Zig Ziglar

Do you have the experience that says, "Oh, I hope that my boss does not come in today at work or forgets to ask me whether the project is complete or not, as I did not finish yet?" Or "Oh, I played the game all afternoon and late at night and I was tired, so I did not finish my homework. I hope our teacher is out today so I can escape getting a bad grade. I told my mom that I finished my project!" Or "I've done other things, but I procrastinated on the most important one, and I lied to my friend who was waiting for the results." Or "I put off writing my book, and I keep doing things that are not important. I procrastinated, and now the deadline is approaching, and the book is not complete!"

We all relate to these things daily—white lies, irresponsibility, not keeping our word—and it takes our motivation and confidence away. Part of this problem is motivation, a mindset problem, and not being clear about what you want! It's about discipline and laziness. To motivate yourself and see farther than your feet is very important when you try to create a better life for yourself and those around you. Depending on your belief system, I guess there could be more truth in that statement. Of course, having integrity does not mean there is no room for error or that a person of integrity is always picture-perfect in every word, thought, or deed. At work or in relationships, a person of integrity will most certainly hold to this value regardless of the situation. So, when it comes to professional relationships and personal relationships, too, for that matter, I watch people's actions and see if their words align. Those that don't are the ones who are showing you who they are by their actions. These individuals will more than likely make bad choices, usually at someone else's expense.

First, I would recommend seeing the root of these problems, being aware of the blind spots we all have, and switching from being ordinary to being extraordinary and not falling for mediocrity. By living with integrity and being a person of your word and planning your work/working your plan, you open yourself to the whole realm of possibilities to explore what it means to be a high achiever with integrity. When we live with integrity, we don't have to live in fear that someone will catch us since we have nothing to hide, and we do not have to feel guilty, as guilt is an emotion that suppresses our sense of deserving and fulfillment.

ACTION STEPS

To sustain the integrity in our lives and to be a person/executive of your word, ask yourself these questions:

- What do I know how to do?
- What am I saying I will do?
- What do others expect me to do?
- What do I have to do to have my work complete?
- What do I need to do in a way to be done?

- What are my values?
- What do I stand for?

When we live with integrity in our own lives, it will affect our own lives and the lives of our family, of those in our workplace, and in our relationships. As it has been said, "How we do one thing is the way we do everything." Integrity is your honesty, your moral character, and your ability to make ethical decisions. Integrity also describes your accountability and willingness to accept responsibility for your actions and decisions. Whether it's our family, business, or work where we maintain healthy relationships with those we lead, we must act with integrity. Integrity inspires trust within your family, with your colleagues, and in your relationships. Once trust is lost, it's hard to ask people to trust you again. If we do not own these qualities, people will experience disgust and shame, and feel confusion, betrayal, and rejection. It's essential to maintain integrity in the workplace. You don't want to create doubt in the minds of your employer, coworkers, and clients. If we don't trust ourselves, no one else will trust us either. Without integrity, we live a life of disgrace and dishonesty. Do you take your integrity to work with you? Integrity will create a sense of comfort for people who entrust you with them. People will rely on you to make the right decisions. Clients will trust their funds to you. Integrity is something we can learn, develop, and strengthen over time. In my experience, it works if you work at it. Life experience is the best teacher of integrity.

I found a coach who I know has high standards of integrity. I picked her brain and learned from her. How is she behaving? How does she deal with a lack of integrity in others? I believe that if one is willing to look inside oneself and cultivate the qualities of curiosity, honesty, and integrity, qualities we all have, and act this way in business and our personal affairs, the world would be a much better place to live. One of the immense opportunities for productivity improvement comes from improving the interpersonal relationships among team members. Questions like these help uncover problems and opportunities to help every person become a better team member.

- Whom on the team do you have the most difficulty working with? Why?

- How would you describe the work environment on the team? Is it more competitive or collaborative?

- How could we improve the way our team works together?

- Who is kicking ass on the team? What have they done?

- Who do you admire on the team? Why?

- Do you feel the team and Why hear your ideas?

- Who would you like to work with more often? Why?

- Is everyone pulling their weight on the team?

- Do you help other members of the team? Do others help you when you need it?

- What's one thing we should change about how our team works together?

- What characteristics make someone a good fit for our team? How would you look for those characteristics in an interview?

- What's the biggest thing you'd like to change about our team?

- What do you like most about working on our team?

- Has anyone on the team ever made you feel uncomfortable? What happened?

One-on-one is an excellent time to coach people on issues they're having with integrity or coworkers. You can also use it as an opportunity to uncover problems in any toxic behavior on the team before they blow up into a big deal. High-performance leaders plan the strategy, monitor it, and manage it to remain aligned with what they want to achieve. Remember the famous words of Peter Drucker: "Culture eats strategy for breakfast."

Listen with curiosity; speak with honesty.
Act with Integrity!

— Roy T. Bennett

CHAPTER 22

Know How Powerful You Are & Leverage Your Power

There is a world within - a world of thought and feeling and power; of light and beauty, and although invisible, its forces are mighty.
— Charles Haanel

How many times do we feel powerless? How many times do we not realize our power?

Often, we forget that we are divine beings with a beautifully soft and precious soul. We are the beauty in the land, and we are here to explore our inner light and strengths. However, we often disconnect ourselves from ourselves and are not aware of how we go through life mostly in our fight-or-flight mode. We think thoughts that are poison or life taken for our wellbeing. For one to be a powerful human is to recognize that within us is the power of breathing in. As long as we breathe and are self-aware of our thoughts and choose to think powerful and positive thoughts, one lives a life in alignment with oneself. When we align with ourselves rather than organically, we align with the outside world as everything reflects our being and reflects us. Think potent thoughts, and you will have powerful feelings, and therefore a powerful life.

How many times do we give our power to anyone?

Don't give your power away. That means yourself out, as you will regret it all your life. The only thing you could provide and is free in life is love, so give love freely. When you do so, what happens is that love bounces back to you, as explained in the law of attraction. No one wants to be in a place to feel powerless, but we will feel that way as long as we do not take one hundred percent responsibility for our lives and recognize that no one could help us if we do not allow ourselves to be helped, as no coach, coworker, or family member can help you if you are not open to change, accept responsibility, and move to a place of love and gratitude. As we know, our feelings are created from the thoughts we think, so be selective in the way you choose your thoughts, and you will be happy, healthy, and wise; a person that anyone would love to have around. Recognize how powerful you are for yourself and choose to be the one, as one cannot be a leader for others before he is a leader for himself. You can feel the whole world within and reach the higher self and not let anything bother you no matter what! Our soul is the most precious thing we have, and we acknowledge and nurture that beauty and divine.

You align with yourself and your community and use the beautiful inner power to serve and be in service for your institution and organization. As one can imagine, we are an electron within the molecule, and therefore we are part of family, organization, community, city, country, world! We cannot operate just by ourselves. We realize that if one electron in the molecule is not in alignment within the cell, the cell cannot function well; by elaborating that our family, organization, community, company, city, country, and world does not work well. That brings us to the realization that to survive and thrive as humankind, we have a duty to our cell and give it all in the most positive way and use our power within for healthy and thriving relationships and human progress of all kinds. I found out that we use the law of attraction without realizing it throughout my life. Developing the self-awareness of this energy field is critical as the hardest thing in the world to do; as Benjamin Franklin explained, "There are three things extremely hard: steel, a diamond, and to know one's self." The emotions we experience drive our lives, and we are often unaware of our blind spots to not see ourselves fully. By developing that consciousness and emotional intelligence that is critical in our development, we catch ourselves into not applying the success principles that drive us powerless. That is the reason that by practicing meditation and breathing exercises daily, we are choosing to be open to our self-awareness and see our blind spots. By doing that, we gain the wisdom that our society is craving for by accepting ourselves with our unique blueprint and getting others in a way they are and looking for the ways you could positively contribute for the greater good.

From the beginning of time, we humans stay together, so knowing we strive to see every way possible to open new windows every day in our mind to the realm of possibility and inclusiveness is how we thrive as human civilizations. Self-awareness is knowing yourself: I clearly understand my emotions and how I react to difficult situations. I know the "triggers" and "stressors" in my life and plan to process stress and disappointment. I continue to stay curious and frequently take steps to learn more about myself. When I receive criticism, I ask: "How can I learn from this experience?" Self-awareness is working with others.

I have a clear understanding of people's emotions and how people react in different environments.

I tailor the way I provide feedback to others based on their innate behavioral drives and needs.

I regularly ask others to give me feedback about my actions, communication, and management style.

I establish a baseline of owed respect.

Every employee should feel that his or her dignity is recognized and respected. It's essential for lower-level workers. Know how to convey respect in your particular workplace. Whether we are leaders or coworkers, we can all shape an environment where colleagues reinforce respectful cues and make social worth a day-to-day reality for one another. For leaders, delegating important tasks, remaining open to advice, giving employees the freedom to pursue creative ideas, taking an interest in their nonwork lives, and publicly backing them in critical situations are some of the many behaviors that impart respect. Recognize that respect has ripple effects. Leadership behaviors are "mimicked" throughout an organization, and incivility can spiral. The cascade from the top down is also likely to shape the way employees treat customers, industry partners, and members of the community. Perhaps you've set a goal that requires a lot of collaboration and cohesion, warranting greater emphasis on owed respect. Conveying respect doesn't necessarily come at the expense of critical tasks. Respect is mainly about how you do what you're already doing. Owed respect is best embedded in our regular interactions and can be as simple as communicating and listening in appreciative ways. Being present to others and affirming others' value to the company should guard against earned respect that is not deserved; it won't resonate. The answers to this feedback you get can also allow you to organize time-specific initiatives and changes within the company. Are they on the edge of burnout or feeling happy and energized? Does the new product launch stress them? Perhaps you should postpone hack day until things settle so that they have space to access their most creative ideas. Employee satisfaction is a precursor to success and accomplishment. When your team is happy, they not only come up with better solutions, but their satisfaction also helps to build an organizational culture of high performance and low turnover.

Evaluate Your Strengths, Rephrase, Renew, Rebuild

CHAPTER 23

The Attitude of Gratitude Operating System

Gratitude: Develop an Attitude of Gratitude; Say Thank You to Everyone you Meet for Everything They Do for You.
— Brian Tracy

I found out that from the moment I open my eyes in the morning, I feel it is a miracle. Before I put my feet on the floor, I thank heaven and all people for the experience they gifted to me, and I am 24/7 grateful for being in this life and have experiences and feelings of this beauty we call life. How my times a day do you feel the gratitude in your heart that starts from the moment you get up until you go to sleep?

As humans, we are prone to habits, and our survival mode gets the upper hand more often than not! Many of us have trained ourselves to complain about what we don't have or don't get. When we don't receive the bounty—and then feel anything but gratitude—we feel resentment and anger instead. It is important to make gratitude a part of our daily life. Having an "attitude of gratitude" uplifts our mood and helps us see the positive side of our lives and create the positive changes we desire. Be grateful for what you have, not what you don't have, and appreciate what you have. Much of having an attitude of gratitude involves training ourselves to feel thankful and regularly see the good in our lives. Having tools and techniques to practice daily helps us change our perspective and the results we achieve daily. Optimism and critical thinking are skills that can be cultivated and one of the ways to develop it is to think, feel, and express gratitude both for the small and the big things that take place in your life.

A gratitude attitude paves the way to your peace of mind as well. Gaining peace of mind is an ongoing, continuous experience that takes time to cultivate, primarily because it involves self-work in learning to work with and become mindful of your thinking and thoughts which negative thinking patterns can dissolve. In their place, new, supportive patterns of positive thought can grow. The attitude of gratitude exercise helps you cultivate peace. Prepare your mind to receive new possibilities and potential; experience the benefits of an attitude of gratitude today.

A research study found that a grateful heart is a healthy heart. In this investigation, patients who viewed their first heart attack as a blessing in disguise for giving them a new appreciation for life were less likely to have a second attack than those who blamed their heart's troubles on others. We will be better parents, better leaders and show an attitude of gratitude in our children and employees by explaining to them that how much thought, time, love, and energy a person spends is the gift of their time and goods. We forget to do these things; we don't take the time, so this is just another way of having an attitude of gratitude—expressing gratitude for being alive another day. If you take that moment and think of how many things in a minute we touch, see, feel, and eat, the gratitude is endless, and you will live a satisfying life. Find some good for which to offer up thanks to God, or whatever you call the Higher Power.

The Attitude of Gratitude exercise: You will need a paper or a journal/notebook for a gratitude journal and a pen, pencil, or particular writing utensil.

- Bless your stress. Assess your body, your mind, your heart, your spirit.
- Reflect on the day and be thankful for the air you breathe.
- Reflect on feeling thankful for what you have. Feel the feeling of thankfulness and gratitude within you.
- It's a most potent exercise to offer gratitude for these things as if you were experiencing them right at the moment. Say, "I am so grateful for the job I just landed."
- Say, "I am so grateful for the wonderful health I am now experiencing," or feel grateful for desire itself.
- What do you notice about yourself: your body, mind, heart, and spirit?
- Have thanks for having returned safely to your bed, having achieved something during the day.
- Gratefulness will help you to see and feel all of the magic around you consciously.
- You can be grateful for the big things and small things. It's great to go to sleep feeling grateful.

In Jewish tradition, the first prayer each morning is gratitude for our soul, returned to our body after sleep, and working for all the parts of our body.

Vocalizing our intentions to manifest things in the future provides a beautiful vehicle for actually having them manifest in our lives. And the best way to allow these beautiful gifts into our experiences lies in affirming that they already are coming to us. Make it a rule to come up with at least five journal entries per day. Each day spend time being grateful for things you don't yet have but that you desire. Act as if you know they have already manifested in your life. A great time to do this is in the morning and the evening with your other gratitude prayers. The more specific you get about these goals and desires, the better.

ACTION STEPS

Stress relief tips can help you change. Take a moment. Fertilize your wellbeing using this stress relief tip, the Attitude of Gratitude exercise. Weed your negative patterns with this simple and good therapeutic remedy: the healing art of giving thanks. Yes. Saying *thank you* is medicinal.

- I asked myself what it means to have a grateful heart. I realized that it begins by reflecting and contemplating on gratitude. Having a thankful heart has to do with a state of being and has to be cultivated by self-reflection.
- Not only do these invocations make you feel better because they affirm that what you need or want is coming your way, but they also have a way of actually attracting these things into your life.
- A friendly smile, a helping hand, the elevator held open, an opening for you to move in traffic, a compliment, someone turning in work on time.
- Some people might find these tips a bit difficult, especially if they find themselves in severe straits.
- To help these people move from feeling like they don't have what they want and need to a place of gratitude.
- Or move from feeling anger and resentment over not having something to feeling excitement over the possibility of having it.
- We have to learn to be happy—to change our energetic vibration—to receive what we want. We do that with gratitude by being happy and thankful for what we already have and have coming to us.
- We may not realize that gratitude is a choice and doesn't come easily to many of us.

- Most of us were taught as children to say "thank you" when someone gave us a present or did something nice for us. After a while, the thank you can become quite glib unless we learn ways to cultivate the attitude of gratitude.
- The children themselves are then less likely to say *thank you* out of obligation or rote and can say thank you from a grateful heart.
- Model this yourself and let your children know that you are grateful for them and are thankful for everything in your life. Children notice and are aware of everything, and they will imitate whatever you do so that they will learn from your example.
- Gratitude is also a skill, and it is never too late to learn a skill. Teach your children that it only takes a moment of opening their eyes to see all the blessings around them. Each night before they go to bed, they can ask themselves this question: What am I grateful for today?
- When you are in a state of gratitude, you resonate and send out a frequency of acceptance and harmony. As a result, you resonate at a much higher vibrational frequency, attracting you to the events, conditions, and circumstances you desire.
- The truth is, it is not easy to be grateful when the things in your life go wrong. But you know what? If you manage to develop deep down inside yourself the attitude of gratitude daily, the universe will respond the way you don't even expect, no matter how you're doing.

I love this quote from my mentor Jack Canfield: "If you don't make this kind of choice, you will find yourself missing all the magical moments of your life."

- Start developing the attitude of gratitude and feel more creativity along the way. You will be astonished how the attitude of gratitude will make you feel more fulfilled in your life.

- Do you have problems with your sleeping? Well, the moment you hit the bed in the evening, try to close your eyes, smile, and start to analyze your day. Be grateful for what the whole day has brought you. Take six deep breaths. This activity will get you a restful sleep, I can promise.

When it comes to the attitude of gratitude, you must know that the habit of practicing gratitude can help you become a positive person.

If you help three people and those three people each help three people, you see where this is going. Gratitude has a ripple effect. Please pass it along.

ACKNOWLEDGMENTS

This book would not exist without everything I have learned from my mentors and professors, Barry Honig and Andrea Califano. Thank you for your friendship, care, leadership, and generosity and for continuing to be the source of knowledge and strength for me.

Thank you to my extraordinary love one, who introduced me to the love, ideas, skills, and personal example of being exceptional. Thank you for the tremendous support, for stretching me, encouraging me, and for pouring your soul into creating a powerful human being. I thank you for believing in me when I did not believe in myself and believing in who I have become in the process.

Thank you to my mentor, Jack Canfield, for taking me step-by-step into becoming a high performer and a success trainer without burning out. Thank you for your generosity, excellence, integrity, and empathy. Thank you to my coach, Mary Morrissey—the coach of my soul.

Thank you to the fantastic leaders—Mark Anderson, John Almandoz, Conner Neil, Barry Teri, Chip Massey, Hope Rothenberg—who helped me most significantly in every area in which a person can grow.

Thank you to my parents for being my inspiration and light in life, teaching me the fundamentals of being a powerful human, and nurturing my heart and mind so I could thrive even in the most rigid ways of living under the totalitarianism of Albanian communism.

Thank you to my sisters for being the best sisters and friends in the world, as you are the ones anyone would dream of having.

Thank you to my son Arthur who removed all the burdens from me, as he grew up faster than he should have to be my inspiration, with unconditional love, care, and fueling the fire within me to get me going. I love you to more than words can say, my son.

Thank you to Fred Gencer, my ex-husband, for his generosity, companionship, and never saying "No" to anything I needed.

ABOUT THE AUTHOR

Desi Tahiraj has over 25 years excelling in the government and education industries, and is known as a High Performer who excelled even in the most rigid environment with passion and enthusiasm. She transformed herself from a closed mindset of the 20th century to a growth mindset of the 21st century. She turned around from her burnout, her limitations, and failures, extraordinarily described in her first published book: "Fail & Get Up & Never Give Up!"

As always, passion and enthusiasm for work and family came through. She looked up to learn from her mentor who rejected the rejection, the world-famous Number One Success Coach Mr. Jack Canfield, as he was left 143 times and never gave up his dreams! So, neither did she!

As a high performer, she learned from the USA's best institutions, organizations, and mentors, and now she is a high achiever without burning out! She is passionate about helping everyone who comes across her path.

Desi comes from communist Albania, an isolated and small country, where the communist regime killed twenty-seven members of her family for the single reason that they were not communists. Her family was hit hard by that regime, where they were not allowed to love, marry, be educated, or get jobs.

Now, she is the founder of Desi Tahiraj Consulting Inc., after working as a human resources professional at Columbia University. She gained a business education from Columbia University Business School, ExecuNet Inc. (Mark Anderson); The University of Navara Business School campus in New York City with Prof. John Almandoz; Smith College with Chip Massey; Peter Bregman and Jeff Hyman.

In 2010 and 2011, she received an award for Distinguished Service in Management at Columbia University from Barry Honig. In July 2019, she received The Albert Nelson Marquis Lifetime Achievement Award from Marquis Who's Who.

In July 2020, she received The Top Transformational Coach of the Year 2020 by the International Association of Top Professionals (IAOTP).

She is a proud member of the International Association of Women (IAW) since 2018.

She is a proud member of the Fort Lee NJ Chamber of Commerce.

Desi is the founder and CEO of Improving Human Performance in Business, a consulting firm providing executive and leadership coaching in the greater New York City Area. In her practice, she focuses on creative thinking and helping others to discover innovative solutions. As a courageous woman, spend has spent the last 30 years in many roles within the public, private, and nonprofit business communities. She offers a unique perspective of operating in business in both male and female roles, and in her research, she developed the Unique Methodology Overcoming

Executive Burnout & Bring back into High Performance and New Discovery, which focuses on important issues of self, allowing a safe space for judgment-free communication, which leads to enhanced performance and diversity of excellence and innovation.

She was recently selected as the Top Transformational Coach of the Year by the International Association of Top Professionals (IAOTP) for her outstanding leadership and commitment to the profession.

Desi has received awards and accolades throughout her career and has been recognized for her outstanding leadership and commitment to those she serves. This year she will be considered for a feature article in TIP (Top Industry Professional Magazine) by (IAOTP). She is also being considered for the Empowered Woman Award for 2021. Desi has been recognized and given an Award for Distinguished Service while in her management position at Columbia University. Recently, she was recognized by Marquis Who's Who for their Lifetime Achievement Award.

As the founder and CEO of Desi Tahiraj Consulting Inc., Desi shares her knowledge of Transformational Coaching, Leadership, Team-Building, Performance, Retention, Negotiation, Conflict Resolution, and Training to corporations, institutions, organizations, and small businesses owners. Desi is also a sought-after international speaker and offers various workshops based on leadership/management, team-building, manage and cures for stress and burnout in the workplace.

Desi is passionate about giving back and works with St. Jude Children's Research Hospital as a volunteer fundraiser in her free time.

LAST WORDS

I would like to thank you for reading my book and sharing my journey. I've enjoyed sharing it. As you probably realize, I have not been able to cover everything.

This book is your new journey of recovering from burnout. It is about your trip, and I want to help you with it.

Validations and Takeaway: Have you identified your values and shared them with others? What types of power do your use and when?

Define success on your terms. Your purpose is like a north star, providing direction yet never reacted. It's what you stand for and it acts as a filter for purposing new opportunities. So, I have three amazing bonuses for you:

1. Text me at 201-951-1178, and I will send you one step a week on how to transform your life.
2. Type in the subject line "Burnout – What's Next?" and we will schedule you a free, 40-minute consultation to help you discover how to thrive and be a high performer by turning around your burnout/failures and enhancing your life every day.
3. To find out how you can be part of my high achiever's mastermind group, please schedule a free call at the following link: https://desitahiraj.com/book-in-a-call/

Thank You – Have a Fantastic Day, High Achievers!

Made in the USA
Middletown, DE
14 April 2021